Then & Now
Angela

ANGELA DAVIDSON

Zaccmed

D1077969

Published by Zaccmedia
www.zaccmedia.com
info@zaccmedia.com

Published April 2015

ISBN: 978-1-909824-82-9

British Library Cataloguing-in-Publication Data
A catalogue record for this book is available from the British Library.

Recent photographs of Angela by Derrick Thomson

ACKNOWLEDGEMENTS

I would like to thank Jacqueline Kerr for encouraging me to start to write, and keeping me encouraged over several years as the idea took shape in my head. To Anna Wood who had the courage to take me on-team at Blairmore House, the Ellel Ministries centre in Scotland. For her support, love and care of me in my journey and for the ministry she so willingly provided over the years. To others, who know who they are, who have ministered into my life, I also say a huge thank you.

To many members of the team and friends at Blairmore over the years who have supported, cared and upheld me in some difficult times I am also indebted.

To Peter Horrobin, for his encouragement and vision that this might make a book; thank you, I can still only say I am astounded.

There would be no book without my two mothers who loved me in their own ways, one who gave me life and the other who took on the role of nurture, provision, education and family.

To all those who have made the book a reality, thank you.

And most importantly I give God all the glory, for without Him this book would only be an autobiography.

CONTENTS

FOREWORD

If you have been adopted, had your baby adopted, or become adoptive parents yourselves, then this book will offer you some valuable insights from the eyes and emotions of an adopted child. Angela shares how the experience caused responses deep within her when as a baby she felt abandoned by her mother and how that affected her for a very large part of her life without her even realising it. As we spent time praying with Angela and sharing the truth from God's Word, we saw how The One who is the Giver of all life, our creator God, is able to bring His truth and His love to comfort deep abandonment and loneliness and bring healing and full restoration to all those who connect back to Him and allow Him to heal their pain and loss. He truly is our hope.

In the pages of this book, Angela has given a fascinating account of her life which appears to start with wealth and privilege, and yet it leads to a saga of restlessness and rootlessness, which continues until she realises the only way to peace is to allow Jesus to help her to face the truth of who she is and where she came from, and the reality of all the pain which had so long been denied.

When I first met Angela she had been attending a course at Ellel Ministries Scotland, and she was offering to help us on the team. She was willing to do anything, and that certainly proved true as over the following years she put her hand to the plough and supported us through some very challenging times as the ministry became established at Blairmore House in Scotland. As she was offering to help, she was completely unaware that she herself might have any need of personal healing. It was only as she spent time serving in the ministry and amongst our family that she saw the plumb line of God's Living Word being practically applied and lived out, that a deep inner heart cry began to stir.

Being amongst family and watching the interaction, the fun, love, and sharing of meals, started to open up a completely new world for Angela and she began to realise a new normality that she never had herself or even seen modelled. This became challenging for Angela and presented her with a choice: to do what she had always done when things became difficult – run away and start again. Or finally to stop running and allow her Heavenly Father to bring His truth, love and comfort into the starved and abandoned place inside. The fundamental need of every human life is human love and nurture. Being handed over for adoption, for whatever reason, however well intended, causes a break in a most precious, life giving relationship of mother and baby, and that inevitably creates a cavern of deprivation and self-abandonment. The unconditional love, acceptance and nurture that every child is created to need, had been lost to Angela. From that time on she had to 'survive' on her own without any expectation of love on her part. Whatever life was to hold for her she decided she had to look after herself.

As time went on as part of Ellel Ministries, Angela began to see how she had built up a highly controlled protection system of independence and self-reliance to protect herself somewhere deep inside from any further rejection.

Gradually, Angela walked the journey of healing through acceptance of the truth, forgiving those who had caused her loss and pain, and receiving God's healing love in the very core of her being. This opened up the way for her to enter into the fullness and abundance of life that only Jesus can bring. It is such a joy and delight to see Angela today, living out her destiny and rejoicing in her restoration. This book brings hope to all who have been touched by adoption.

Anna Wood
Director of Ellel Ministries Scotland, 2000–2014

ANGELA THEN

chapter one

THE SEARCH FOR A BABY

February 1941 was not an easy time for a lone woman to drive from the north-east of England to London in search of a baby girl to adopt. The country was in the midst of war. Blackout was law. There were no visible lights at night in houses and certainly no street lights. The road signs had been removed to prevent the enemy, should they land, from knowing where they were. Rationing of food was strict. Petrol was rationed and almost unobtainable.

Angela's adoptive mother-to-be, aged forty, had given birth to a son, David, in 1938. His father was an eminent Harley Street Ear, Nose and Throat surgeon, and David was the result of a short relationship and a few nights in Brighton. Horrified by the consequences, Doris Lucy, as I shall call her, or DL, somehow persuaded her Jewish boyfriend, Carew (as DL called him), to marry her. In fact, she bought the engagement ring, a lovely big diamond, herself.

It seems that Carew was not prepared to give up his hard-won place on Harley Street, which was understandable. But DL felt she was not prepared to forgo her family home and estate nor the life to which she had become accustomed in order to live in London, which was alien to her. So she returned to her elegant home in the north of England.

Smelt House had been the family residence for several generations and was the only home DL had ever had. Her identity was closely linked with it, and also her relatives and friends all lived around the area. She enjoyed a sort of social significance, with her role as landowner. She was, in effect, the matriarch of a small village her Quaker family had lived in for many generations. So she and Carew were married in name only and lived two completely separate lives in different parts of the country.

David was born with great difficulty in May 1938 and DL was strongly advised by the medical profession not to have more children – hence the reason for the trip to London in blackout.

Leaving David at home with the staff and 'borrowing', perhaps 'stealing' would be more apt, petrol from the Women's Voluntary Service of which she was the local president, DL set off alone in early February, travelling some 200 miles in search of a baby girl to adopt and to be a companion for David. As there were few vehicles on the roads, places to stop and refuel were sparse, as were places to eat; also, cars in those days had no heaters. So it was truly courageous to undertake such a journey alone, especially in wartime.

On entering London and driving to her destination, which was a flat lived in by Carew, she saw only one black cat, but no one out and about. The following day, a visit to the adoption society did not produce the sought-after child. Evidently all the suitable 'white' ones had been sent down to Cheltenham, many miles west of London; in effect, evacuated. Having come this far, DL was not about to return empty-handed, so she journeyed down to Cheltenham and found a bed for the night in an hotel. She was surprised next morning to find that she had slept through an air raid.

A visit to the adoption home found a choice of children, but how does one choose from the array? DL's criteria seems to have included firstly a girl, and for her to have blue eyes. If the potential babies had their eyes shut they were awoken with a smack on the bottom. This process revealed one in particular who met the criteria, so, rather like she was on a shopping trip, DL said, 'I'll take this one.' The baby had been born on 4 February 1941 and records showed that she was in good health.

The infant had been brought to the home on 10 February by her mother and grandmother. However, some four days after being in the adoption home, the baby was not well enough to travel; she was not thriving.

Undaunted and determined to have that child, DL returned north to await a call that the baby was well enough to fetch. Nearly a month passed until the call came. So, accompanied this time by a nanny, DL set off again on more 'borrowed' petrol! The baby was duly collected and driven north to be welcomed to her new home and brother, David. The local rector's wife who visited shortly after exclaimed, 'Why did you bring her home? She will never live!' Quite a pronouncement on the young life.

The baby was christened, which was unusual for a Quaker family, with the name Angela Doris (although her birth mother would call her Gillian). In this affluent household, Angela wanted for nothing, even food, as Smelt House was part of a large estate with a home farm that produced milk, eggs, bacon. The large garden with nine greenhouses produced fruit and vegetables, even peaches and grapes. There were staff although it was wartime, and always someone to keep an eye on the children. Even so, Angela did not do well, she was knock-kneed, had strange toes, and barely any hair. They rubbed olive oil on her scalp but to no avail. She was prone to nosebleeds on a daily basis, and particularly to bouts of bronchitis.

Relations with David seemed trouble-free, David being delighted with the appearance of a sister and companion in naughtiness. There was a huge garden to play in, including a pond with newts with which Angela spent much time playing; there was a swimming pool, where DL used to throw frogs at Angela, because that made the child scream with fear; the nearness of a frog terrified Angela for years.

There were hens to feed and a goat which Angela was convinced was a giraffe when her pram was placed beneath its face and long billy goat beard, which was silhouetted against the blue sky. There were pet rabbits – Angela's was called Snowball, and one day it ended up as lunch with no apology or explanation.

There was a stream of well-intentioned but very elderly, mainly female relatives, so David rarely saw a male. His father only came on one visit north for David's fifth birthday, otherwise the boy had to take trips to London to visit him. Angela has an enduring memory of sitting on Carew's knee at David's birthday party, and thereafter no recollection of any birthday parties for either David or herself until her twenty-first. There was one lovely great-uncle, DL's mother's brother, a bachelor who joined the family for lunch every Sunday after the Quaker meeting – Angela adored him. He smoked a pipe and after lunch Angela was allowed to climb on a chair to reach his pipe and tobacco out of a drawer in the tallboy. She would then fill his pipe and light a match so he could smoke it. This was almost the highlight of the week.

David's attendance at the local school was not a happy start to his education, and DL felt the family would be better off in Darlington, some twelve miles away, where there was a local school founded by Quaker relatives. In 1945, DL rented a large house called Shelley's from one of the relations, so the family and entourage moved in. David attended Polam Hall School and Angela followed just before she was five. The pair were driven to and from school each day, the car having been lovingly cleaned and finished with black boot polish by the chauffeur. Car polish had not then been invented, and all cars were the same colour – black.

Above the age of seven, the school was only for girls, so the dilemma arose of where David would go to preparatory school. There was still rationing and the available clothes coupons would have been insufficient to kit David out for a boarding preparatory school. Knowing nothing about education but determined her son would have the best available, DL set about buying a Georgian house in the middle of a nearby village. She engaged a headmaster and started a preparative school. Hurworth House School for boys opened its doors in 1948 and continued until 2011. DL said near the end of her life that this was her most important achievement.

David attended Hurworth and with some difficulty, aged thirteen, managed to obtain a place at the Quaker school, Leighton Park School in Reading where his uncle, who had unfortunately died in a climbing accident in his early twenties, had studied. David had discovered by then that if he complained to his mother he could get out of playing games or come home early, and so began a lifetime of control and manipulation which became the pattern of his life, in Angela's opinion. Angela, meanwhile, was thoroughly enjoying school and doing quite well, top of the class or near it; she took part in everything on offer and was a good athlete. This was the scene until about the age of nine, when she was thrown out of art class and asked not to sing – only to open her mouth. She was also advised by piano, violin and cello teachers that she was not much use, and by maths and Latin (in which she got 6 per cent in an exam) teachers that she may as well give up. School was increasingly becoming a more negative experience for her.

David was a lonely chap who never had friends, and spent much time in his bedroom making faces at himself in a mirror. He really did not play or have fun; he seemed to be isolating himself and becoming more troubled.

In 1950 the bombshell dropped. One night at bedtime, DL came and sat on Angela's bed, which was not totally unusual, but somehow Angela detected something was different. DL told Angela that she was adopted, which to Angela, who had no idea about matters pertaining to procreation, sounded quite exciting and made her something different. Without a pause she rushed into David's room and announced the fact that she was adopted, and without waiting for a response rushed out again. The damage was done, and the relationship between David and Angela deteriorated with David entering into increased isolation and strange behaviours, with Angela apparently unaffected by this news. David was ever more unable to be the playmate and friend she needed and longed for.

Companions for Angela were limited, as private school friends did not live nearby, so hours and hours were spent alone in all weathers playing tennis against a wall, pogo sticking, walking on stilts, and helping the gardener, or the maids. The resulting activities created a physically well-coordinated body but also an independent and lonely child.

DL was determined that the children would be shown the whole of the British Isles. Every Easter and summer they embarked by car, accompanied usually by a nanny, to a host of locations in Britain, staying in luxurious hotels, often with no other children around, an odd collection of single parent, retainer and two lonely children. DL did as she set out to do, and by the time they were teenagers, they had truly visited almost all areas of the British Isles. There were too many castles and historic buildings for Angela's taste – she wanted more action and excitement. Single parents were not the norm in those days, so it was courageous and bold for DL to take the children away alone, as it must have been a lonely and challenging time for her. She must have endured many strange responses from people.

Sometimes, though, there would be the Pullman train trip to London to see Carew. It was always with some excitement that they watched the shiny train with 'Pullman' written all over it pull into Darlington station, and then to find that Nanny and Angela travelled second class and David and DL went first class – which didn't matter at the time, as the trip was exciting and London would be fun. The distinction, however, did have a lasting, deep effect on Angela.

Carew's secretary, a formidable lady called Miss Leader, would collect the family in the Bentley and off they would go to Harley Street to await the great man! He would appear with an intimidating instrument around his forehead for looking down people's throats, as he was an ENT specialist. They would then be driven by Carew to lunch at either the Ritz or Claridge's, both the most staid and unlikely places for lunch for two children. No play here; only best behaviour! At the end of lunch, two old-fashioned £5 notes – the big, white transparent ones – were placed on the table, one for each child; no hug, no touch, no acceptance, no love, nothing – only a £5 note. They were then dropped back at Brown's Hotel in Dover Street to while away the rest of the day. How DL must have felt on these occasions is almost impossible to imagine, but the children probably thought that was how families were. They rarely, if ever, saw a proper, functional family that showed signs of affection. If they did, they probably thought them strange! The Quaker cousins were not a hugely effective demonstration of family.

Many years later, when Angela visited Carew in London, he was to tell her that he only signed the papers for her adoption to keep DL quiet, which only added to the sense of being rejected, unwanted, marginalised and worthless. In almost the same breath he said if she wasn't his daughter, the situation on that occasion might be different. As Angela was staying in his flat she could only assume one thing! DL was not amused about Angela staying with him and, in fact, she may well have had real concern. But Angela thought DL's reaction was one of jealousy.

chapter two

EARLY YEARS AND SCHOOL

David went off to Leighton Park aged thirteen, and Angela was left at home attending Polam and enjoying school and life in a strange, isolated adult female world. Angela had always been told she would follow DL and three other of her ancestors to the Quaker Mount School, York when she was thirteen. She had attended Old Scholar weekends there with DL since she could remember and had always been excited by the thought of a boarding school. It was with considerable disappointment that age thirteen came and went and there was no move, no mention of The Mount. Early in 1954 Angela developed the annual bout of bronchitis, took a long time to get over it, and stubbornly refused to go back to school. DL must have thought this strange and realised there was a broken promise.

Finally Angela entered The Mount in September 1954. The summer had been punctuated with the excitement of getting the uniform and sewing on name tapes and wondering what it would all be like. Angela had said if there were not properly cooked boiled eggs for the first meal she would come home. There were barely warm boiled eggs for her first supper (and every Sunday breakfast for the next four years) but Angela did not go home. Interestingly, Angela stopped biting her nails the day she went to The Mount. Joining in a year late was not easy as friendships and bonds had already been formed, some since the age of eleven, so there was an element of her being an intruder. That soon passed and the excitement of having escaped from the dreary isolation of home was replaced by the challenges of a new life. Suddenly it dawned on her that lots of people had two parents, who came to take them out on the rare times they were allowed out; this was a real revelation. DL managed on several occasions to be unable, unwilling or whatever to come to York, which was only forty-eight miles from Darlington. However, she always seemed to manage to catch a train to London and go to see David. Angela would run down to the railway bridge by the playing field at school if she had free time and wave to DL as she passed by on her train south.

The holidays were a time of acute loneliness, as it seemed David was withdrawing more and more into himself and was reluctant and unable to participate in family life, which DL tried so hard to provide. It felt like holidays had to be tailored to David's needs and his increasingly difficult and strange behaviour. David struggled through A-levels with poor grades, so went to a crammer and retook them with better results. Conscription for the forces was a heavy cloud over one summer as David was now eligible. He had never made a commitment to the Society of Friends, being from a Quaker family, which meant he would be a Conscientious Objector with all that that entailed. Somehow the issue was resolved and David went off to a teacher training college near London. It was during this time that he became seriously ill while on teaching practice. With a marked stammer and a cultivated accent he was the laughing stock of the inner-city children he was sent to teach. Finally DL provoked a reluctant Carew into action and David was admitted to a psychiatric hospital near London, where he was diagnosed with schizophrenia. It is hard to imagine how DL must have felt, her precious only son diagnosed with a mental health problem with all the stigma attached.

She must have felt a sense of despair and acute isolation as she was too ashamed to share this information with her friends.

Now began the 'revolving door' syndrome which lasted until his eventual incarceration in the Retreat in York in 1978, where he remains in one of its satellite facilities until this day. During the years of David's deterioration the uncertainty, the fear and the shame took its toll on DL. There was always the uncertainty as to his status and when the next crisis would occur. One can only guess at what must have gone on inside DL, with no support from anyone. At some points she was required by the psychiatrist to be in attendance when David had the traumatic electroconvulsive therapy (ECT), a treatment given under anaesthetic for psychiatric disorders. He had eighteen of these treatments. David was subjected to far more than was considered normal. The housekeeper and staff were increasingly afraid of his presence as he was prone to bouts of violence, or spent days in his room in the dark; meals were missed and personal hygiene forsaken. There was a thankful respite when he was hospitalised or returned for short spells to London.

Angela, meanwhile, was enjoying the challenge of The Mount, and although her grades had not kept up their early promise, she managed some O-levels, aged sixteen. She arrived back at school to do A-levels and was greeted by the second head who asked why she was there, to which Angela replied, 'To do A-levels.' This was met with, 'I don't think so!' A forbidden phone call home galvanised DL to action; she caught a train and came in all her indignation to stand up for Angela and demand her right to stay. The case was won and Angela stayed on and studied geography and biology to Advanced level, and to the surprise of most people, passed them both. It seems that after the adoption announcement her grades had dropped. Her memory was always a limitation; where others could read and remember it was rote learning, which was a burden for Angela. However, tennis, hockey and team play offset the academic disappointments. The school encouraged development in many spheres and there were plenty of extracurricular activities. Angela was popular and made long-term friends. She was an active and enthusiastic participant in most things and took her responsibilities as a prefect very seriously.

The ethos of The Mount gave Angela a solid grounding in service to others; there was an expectation of putting others before self. 'To those God giveth much the more requireth He' was an often-quoted verse from Scripture, as was the school motto 'Faithfulness in little things'. The school song, based on Psalm 127, 'Except the Lord the city keep, the watchmen watch in vain' resonated through Angela's life. There was no encouragement, or really desire, or probably ability on Angela's part to go to university, so what to do? The question arose one summer holiday and DL said, 'Stay home and arrange the flowers.' Well, that did it, the vision of flowers like T.S. Eliot's coffee spoons stretching out before her made a decision a must. So why not go and train for institutional management at Atholl Crescent in Edinburgh, a well-known and well-regarded college? So in September 1958, the trunk packed the train taken – no car ride offered! – Angela set off for Edinburgh. Independence beckoned, and a life full of new challenges, friends, activities and learning, but not too academic.

Edinburgh was wonderful; the course was not stretching at all which was a real relief after the struggle of A-levels. The people were fun, interesting, and Edinburgh life posed all sorts of new excitements to be savoured. One of the first lessons at college was how to use a vaccum cleaner, which Angela thought was a huge joke. She had watched the 'Hoover' man, who came every year to the house to maintain the cleaner, so she not only knew how to use one but how to service it. New skills, making leather gloves, cooking strange-sounding Scottish meals like minced collops, served on an ashet. Ironing a shirt had to take forty-five minutes and a handkerchief, five minutes. This put Angela off for life. As the year progressed it became apparent that hot kitchens and heavy pans were not the ticket for Angela. Previously she had thought of housing management or estate management but felt there would be too much maths involved. A colleague was going on to do occupational therapy, whatever that was, but it sounded like fun and not too academic. Pursuing the idea, Angela found that one of the cousins was an OT in Durham, so a visit was arranged in the holidays. Taken with the idea, the cousin pulled strings to get Angela into Dorset House in Oxford, an occupational therapy college, in the autumn. An interview was arranged in Oxford to which DL and Angela went, with acceptance forthcoming.

chapter three

THE OXFORD YEARS AND YOUNG ADULTHOOD

Oxford here we come. Angela was a year later than most starting so she was able to be in digs, a private home renting rooms to students and providing breakfast and dinner. A room with a total stranger at the same college and a bike ride from Dorset House was a challenge indeed. Pilchards in tomato sauce for breakfast once a week gave Angela a lifetime aversion to them, and four years of Ryvita and cheddar cheese for lunch was enough. College was very hard, Saturday morning as well and no free periods. There was a bike ride up a long hill every day for some time, until Angela conned DL into buying her a car because of a bad back for which she now wore what can only be described as a torture belt. The back problem was a result of doing too many headstands, falling off bikes and horses head first, as well as some serious falls whilst skiing, and the consequences of a very bad car crash as a child.

The course was great, so many new and creative skills to learn, woodwork, metal beating, weaving, embroidery, cane work, all of which Angela found exciting and in which she excelled. The study of new subjects both in physical medicine and psychiatry were very demanding and the terms were long. The Oxford university undergrads were only there for twenty-four weeks, so some serious work was a possibility when they were away. Many of the new contacts became lifelong friends. The antics of a group of enthusiastic young ladies on the loose can only be imagined, with all the access to Oxford and university life. Hospital practice had them going all over the country to psychiatric and physical medicine hospitals. Time spent in London at King's College Hospital was a highlight for Angela. A flat with six students with two cars and the night-life of a London in full Chubby Checker Twist mode was irresistible. Punting on the River Cherwell, May morning celebrations, commemoration balls at varying colleges, an unforgettable ball at Blenheim Palace, parties in London and elsewhere – but thankfully no visible evidence of drugs.

Angela survived with her virtue intact and qualified as an OT in 1963. Reality now set in; with her salary being a mere £995 per annum, living away from home would be almost impossible. So Angela landed her first job at Middlesbrough General Hospital, about a twenty-five minute drive from Darlington. DL's response to this was: 'If David wants to come home you will have to get out.' More rejection. In reality Angela would want to do just that anyway, though it did reinforce the second-class citizen status. David was living in a Quaker club in London when well enough to do so, or he would land back at home in a dreadful state and be admitted to hospital in Middlesbrough. His father had by now abandoned any responsibility for him so it rested squarely on DL. She was clearly struggling to handle the increasingly desperate situation, and she had felt unable to share the tragedy with her friends. Her friends knew something was wrong as when they enquired they were told David was in London, and if he was home he was not seen. DL was so appalled by his condition and ashamed that she felt quite unable to share the situation, though Angela knew that they knew all was not well. They would have been unable to help anyway. Social services were contacted but just took one look at the size of the house and said no help would be forthcoming. So not even any professional help was offered, and this reinforced her isolation and hopelessness.

Angela was putting flesh on what she had learned and enjoyed her new profession, which in 1965 was still very much in the pioneering stage, actually making the raised toilet seats, and doing the cane seating! There was beginning to be germinated the idea of travel and escape from the increasingly turbulent goings-on at home – a wanting to escape the exclusion and stifling life of David with his problems. There was also a seed growing that said her own mother must be better than DL. This latter thought dominated her thinking, as well as the desire to flee. Thankfully the desire to find her biological mother was discarded at she felt it would have been done for all the wrong reasons and that she was not mature enough to cope with the consequences, whatever they might be. So why not start with Canada and slowly circumnavigate the globe? OT was a passport to the world of work in those days when the British Empire still needed people!

A job was secured at Ottawa Civic Hospital in Ontario, Canada, so a trip to Canada House in London was next. Somehow Angela jumped the queue, as it appeared on that day she was the only white emigrant, not politically correct but that was before PC was invented! Papers in hand, plans for the great adventure could proceed. DL was not happy, as she had expected Angela to look after her in her old age. She was sixty-four now and this girl to whom she had given a home and exposure to a first-class education was abandoning her. DL made that quite apparent, which gave Angela a lasting sense of being beholden to her, in effect being manipulated by her, and a deep sense of guilt at emigrating. A berth was secured on the *Empress of Canada* for 8 October 1964, leaving from Liverpool. DL did travel to see Angela off, as did some friends, but nothing was going to dampen her excitement.

The voyage was appallingly rough. Most of the crew and passengers were sick; not Angela though. She and a man she had met managed the whole voyage upright. Two days late into Montreal, at midnight the great ship docked; thankfully the Salvation Army was there to help – what a blessing they were. Next day Angela travelled to Ottawa and stayed in a friend's flat until getting her own accommodation. Work was demanding, much more so than England; no wasting time and tea breaks here. Travel by bus in freezing temperatures was a challenge, Angela had never done buses! A flat was found and life became a routine for a few months. Angela was visited at weekends by John, the boat acquaintance, or travelled by Greyhound coach many miles up to Thessalon in Northern Ontario. That is where John, aged forty-four to Angela's twenty-four, a widower and mayor of the town, lived with his two sons. The family had been devastated a couple of years earlier by John's wife Margaret's death from cancer, leaving John L, aged six, and Peter, aged twelve. Peter had just been sent to private school in Toronto, an eight-hour drive away, while John attended the local school. John senior was running a very successful insurance business.

Angela at twenty four was very naïve. A real eye-opener for her was to be in the company of men – 'Why on earth do they leave the loo seat up?' David never did because the gent's loo at home had a spring on it, so Angela was unaware of the male habit and their urinating procedure. John's brother-in-law, sister and mother all lived in Toronto, along with his four nephews, so visits there watching a family interact was a revelation. There had been a cautious welcome tempered by obvious concern as to where this relationship might go, due to the age gap. Deep in Angela's heart she knew she was looking for the love she had not received, for a father figure and a family to be part of. Although there was a caution, she was falling in love. Actually, what did love mean to someone who had not experienced it?

The relationship continued apace, and by the year end there were calls home to DL to talk about marriage. DL swiftly without warning put a solicitor on the case to investigate John. The investigation was apparently was not good, so DL suggested Angela return home, obviously thinking Angela was pregnant and at the same time remembering her own dilemma years earlier (about which Angela was then unaware). However, Angela was headstrong, determined, rebellious and, sensing what passed for love, there were plans afoot for marriage. In the event DL called Angela home but John refused to let her go without him. Arriving home to face the music and abject disapproval of John, the couple determined to marry. John told Angela he would give her the best ten years of her life, a curse upon the marriage which was fulfilled. However, John had not brought his wife's death certificate with him so they could not be married in Darlington. The plan was to go to London and see old college friends, who would arrange all. This they did, unaware of the glitch, so in Caxton Hall John signed in as a bachelor with Angela's brother, David, as witness, in one of the rare times of relative sanity. DL showed her disapproval by having a cold so she couldn't travel. Bad choice, Angela! It's called free will.

Married life in Thessalon was fun. It was an interesting small town – Angela was a news story. All wanted to meet the mayor's new wife, gawp and tittle-tattle. Being the mayor's wife had its interesting times. Very soon after arriving, the undertaker, a good friend of John's, died. Attendance at all funerals was a mayoral duty and open coffins were the norm. Suddenly Angela found herself beside the wife of the deceased who was saying, 'Doesn't he look lovely', when she had never seen a dead body – or seen the man alive! The prime minister, Lester Pearson, visited so that demanded decorum and talk of politics of an unknown nature. Weekends were spent in summer on a small lake with a cabin. There were lots of mice, and mosquitoes which had arrow precision on to the rear end if exposed for the necessary loo procedures au natural. However, water skiing with the boys and barbecues were endless fun.

There were some obviously difficult and traumatic times for all. The anniversary of Margaret's death continued to traumatise John; there was great loss and sadness which the boys covered up well, particularly Peter, who was an adolescent and a macho man. Young

John, though, started to show the effects of the unhealed trauma, with consistent bed-wetting, and lowering school grades. Angela had no idea how to deal with his grief and trauma, and with hindsight dealt with it appallingly. Many years later Angela asked young John for forgiveness for her ignorance and treatment. Thankfully John was very eager to forgive and say that he had not been affected – which in reality is not too likely.

John senior was looking for 'pastures green', as he did consistently throughout the marriage. The Bahamas came into focus as he had spent time during the war with the Argyllshire and Sutherland Highlanders in Jamaica, and had holidayed with Margaret in Nassau. John went alone on an exploratory visit to Nassau and rented a house. He arranged to sell up the Thessalon house but leave his business in the hands of his wonderfully competent secretary, Mary. A Volkswagen van was bought and everyone piled in for the long trip south. Well, what a journey – Angela couldn't believe how good things could be. The journey took some time down the east coast of the USA to Miami as the family stopped off in places of interest along the way. The boys in particular enjoyed the trip. The reality of arriving by boat in Nassau, unloading the VW and driving to the new home was so exciting. John had been assured that he would find well-paid work, as he had a long-term friend who lived there. So money did not seem to be an issue.

The very first morning in the local paper was an advertisement for an occupational therapist at the local geriatric hospital attached to the psychiatric hospital. Angela at age twenty-six had not really considered working! So she thought, 'Let's apply and see what happens.' She got the job as there were no other OTs on the island, and so to work. It was a good time and a steep learning curve, particularly working with abandoned multi-handicapped children from the outer islands. The very first day at work, Angela was feeling she had really arrived in the OT world, because for the first time she had a desk and office to herself. Just beginning to explore the office and settle down, her eye caught something moving in the air conditioner. When she examined this closer it proved to be a grass snake. Without considering propriety or anything, she flew out of the office, screaming! A six foot grass snake was removed. Angela always checked the conditioner after that.

chapter four

NASSAU LIFE

That work experience shaped, in many ways, the compassion for abandoned and helpless people in a very two-tiered society. One was of extreme wealth from colonial days and one of profound and intractable poverty from the slave trade years, and the severe and deep wounding of the native Islanders who had been oppressed. The sight of the native population coming out from their straw huts, the children dressed in the whitest of white clothing one had ever seen, on a Sunday morning to worship the Lord had a longstanding and profound effect on Angela. The sound of praise and worship which could be heard was truly amazing when poverty and hopelessness abounded. Just occasionally the family would go to church and join in the powerful times of worship. Life in a hot climate is enervating, and being permanently covered in a layer of dampness was a new phenomenon. The housemaid who came with the rented accommodation was a real treasure and shared her gifts and expertise of cooking the native dishes so willingly. There were new fish to deal with, particularly conch which lived in those lovely big shells and made wonderful conch fritters, and conch salad, fresh tuna fish, either bought or caught, grits, black beans and, of course, wonderful fruit and vegetables.

John got an excellent job working for the insurance arm of the Victor Sassoon organisation, which had its tentacles all over the world. Victor's widow ran the Bahamian outfit with great grace and an iron fist. There were parties at the beach house on Paradise Island long before the bridge was there, starting with a boat trip, then feasting on turtle pie and swimming just offshore with a Styrofoam ring with a gin and tonic stuck in it. Course after course of local food came effortlessly before one, and the day just melted into evening and then night. The international guests were always interesting and a whole new world opened up. There was golf to be played most days on idyllic courses, and a Chris-Craft twin-engine boat, in which the family explored the outer islands with some interesting adventures, one of which was when Angela was steering the boat at somewhat high speed, heading for an island to which they had been numerous times. Unfortunately, account had not been taken of the tides, so suddenly with a sickening thump the boat ground itself onto a coral reef. Nothing to do but wait till high tide, apart from don a snorkel and examine the damage which was a rather deformed propeller!

The reality was that Peter was not doing well at St Andrew's school in Toronto and young John was learning nothing at school in Nassau. Decisions had to be made. Angela pulled some strings and got young John a place in a well-known prep school at Stow-on-the-Wold to which she took him by plane without a passport to England to start the new term, flying back to Nassau after 'abandoning him' in an alien country. He always maintained that he was not damaged by the experience. Peter, again with strings pulled, secured a place at Leighton Park, where generations of Angela's family had been. But Peter discovered the discipline and the academic excellence was beyond his grasp. He descended almost into anarchy and a dismal academic performance, which infuriated his father who knew he was capable of better.

Young John blossomed at his new school and returned home to Nassau with an increasing maturity and self-confidence. Peter, now beginning to show the loss of his mother in his behaviour and with an increasing alienation from his father, had to find out what he should pursue as a career. His father having been in the army, Peter thought he could gain approval by joining an English regiment. He made it to officer training with the Royal Green Jackets in Winchester, one tough infantry outfit. He was found wanting, however, and was demoted from officer training to ordinary training.

The family was now moving to England as the situation in Nassau when the government became an all native one was untenable for both John and Angela. The leaving party for Angela arranged by Lady Sassoon was quite the most spectacular that Angela had ever seen. It was given in the Old Bahamian Club, which was the old colonial casino and meeting place of the mega-wealthy of the day. The array of food, mostly seafood, was piled high on a huge table, the most seafood in one place that Angela had ever seen. It was indeed a send-off, then right away to catch the plane to England. John, who had always wanted to run a pub, had decided this was the time. A pub had been found in Portmellon near Mevagissey, Cornwall to be purchased from the current owner, Lord Gordon of Huntly, Aberdeenshire, Scotland. Angela was dispatched to apply for the licence and open the bar for the season. The season was defined by the fact that the sea came over the road in front for most of the winter, not conducive for trade. Angela became the youngest female publican in the country – what an accolade! The pub was a melting pot of tradespeople from the Midlands, locals and high-flying international tourists, all with strange drink requests, quite unknown to Angela who was just about teetotal in those days. The pace of running a pub which could easily serve two hundred made-to-order sandwiches at lunchtime and a full restaurant at night as well, was demanding in the extreme, so hard work and no slacking were the order of the day. The boys both helped when they were at home – but not a lot. One day while Angela was skinning a Dover sole, the fish shot off the work surface in the kitchen and landed in the bar in front of the guests who had ordered it. Not ideal! Another day, Angela tripped up the steps to the dining room with two plates laden with food which landed firmly on the carpet. Angela made a quick retreat and left the scene to be dealt with by others. She was not seen again that night.

John and Angela had been advised that having children was not on as Angela had a rare blood group which would not match well with John's. This was OK until Angela got broody and sought medical advice that now said 'times have moved on, it's alright'. Angela became pregnant, but after two months all appeared not well and the nurse was sent for and advice given to stay in bed, and she would come daily with an injection. The bed rest was not easy to achieve as the bedroom was right over the bar, and there was a suspicion that if a baby was only kept in place by having an injection, could this be right? And damage was likely. One glorious day with John's blessing Angela could stand bed no more and went for a walk. What freedom! Nothing drastic happened, so a few days later they went for a few days' break at a cottage they had bought on Dartmoor. That's when it happened, the miscarriage, in the middle of the night, in the loo downstairs, alone in pain and bewilderment. Returning to bed, John sleeping, Angela continued the night, and in the morning thought a visit to the doctor appropriate. Unaccompanied, Angela visited the doctor who duly confirmed the situation and sent Angela home to do nothing, horrified that she had driven herself to the surgery. Angela as usual kept on going and decided not to dwell on the issue, so it was well buried.

Life went on at the busy pace but John had tired of the pub life and its demands. It had been a good money earner. John had to go to Canada to see to his business there and Angela was given the task of fetching a brand new motorhome from the middle of London. The pair were going to embark on a trip across Canada and back sailing again on the *Empress of Canada*. The pub now sold, the cottage sold, a corgi dog was found a new home, and the new family home was a

Ford Caravan International motorhome. Peter was back in Canada, having been unceremoniously thrown out of the Green Jacket officer training corps in Winchester and then given a ticket back to Canada by his father. The main reason for his return to Canada was he had made sexual overtones to Angela one weekend when his father was away. On his return, John sensed something was wrong and out came the confession, and a furious John dispatched his son instantly. This episode was never resolved between Peter and his father, and it influenced Angela's relationship with Peter and in future with his wife, whom Peter would tell. Young John was happily at a school in Bideford, Devon, about to move to HMS Conway on Anglesey. This was a training facility for merchant seamen which was to be his chosen and very successful career.

The passage to Montreal was uneventful, the motorhome winched unscathed from the ship, and the journey began. Visits to John's family in Toronto were fun, and then on to Thessalon, still familiar territory. Angela must have been exhibiting some signs of instability following the miscarriage as John insisted she see one of his medical friends in Sault Ste Marie. Nothing much was said, just 'Carry on, but don't try to get pregnant again.' So that's what happened, no grieving, no mention of loss or the inner sadness. A wonderful exciting journey of discovery of that varied country followed, stopping every night in glorious campsites. The prairies seemed to go on forever and the mountains were unforgettable, all the way to Vancouver and its afternoon tea Englishness. The return was cut short – young John was not joining the trip as he needed help to move schools, so he headed for DL and Darlington where he was always welcomed, which was more than his father was.

Flying home and arriving at Heathrow with no vehicle or home was interesting. By the end of day one, a VW campervan had been bought and the trip to Darlington was under way. Young John now joined the party and a foray into Scotland was decided upon, to fill up the remainder of the summer holidays. Actually it was time to give some thought to accommodation and work. Returning south,

York was decided upon as a base. A rental house was found and Angela landed a job managing a health food shop – all the 'in thing' at that point. The money management bit was a struggle for Angela, so John came each evening and totted up the day's takings. That was until he had another brainwave that they would go for four days to Ibiza to investigate a business opportunity. Of course, the business thing was a non-starter, but John decided they should buy a villa and go and live there. Angela, who was still enjoying all the change and constant running away, readily agreed. Of course, all these adventures seemed appealing to her, and she didn't object, though in effect she would not have thought them up on her own.

So began three years of living on Ibiza, right in the middle of the hippy, drug, escape-from-Vietnam-conscription time. Living in a lovely villa up on a hill, Angela, aged about thirty-one, had some really interesting neighbours: one of the Horlicks family, a retired vicar of the Guinness family, and the most wonderful elderly widow lady who had trained horses for the Raj in India – she could keep one riveted for hours with her stories. She was an amazing pianist; sometimes, coming up from the village at night, one could hear her playing, stop the car, and go in and listen, even though she could be quite oblivious to one's presence for ages. Her son was captain of the Royal Yacht *Britannia*, so young John and he would talk sea things. There were exceptional beaches and stunning views. John did a bit of bar work and Angela did nothing much except when the steady stream of visitors came by – a quite idyllic life, but sad, really, to see the creeping expansion of tourism with building encroaching on the indigenous population. There was an old lady who would daily bring her sheep and goats past the house on her way to the pasture and sometimes Angela would engage her in conversation – actually, neither spoke any of the other's language, but Angela was aware of her distress as she was slowly being surrounded by concrete and watching her territory shrink. Her sons were involved in the expansion of tourism so she was torn between her old life and her sons' new wealth.

chapter five

More Wanderings

The next milestone was young John leaving school and heading for a job with Andrew Weir & Co. as a cadet seaman. So it was felt a home was needed in England for when he did return from his six to nine-month stints at sea. The villa was not sold, but John and Angela returned to Britain to rent a house near Nottingham where Angela looked up an old college friend who was heading up an OT department. A job was forthcoming so that sorted the financial side. John was minded to have a hardware store and eventually found suitable premises with a house in a small village near Newark. Angela changed jobs to be nearby and was headquartered in Lincoln, but it covered a lovely part of Lincolnshire from Horncastle. The shop was not a great success as a big DIY store and similar stores were taking over from small shops. There were fascinating trips to hardware wholesalers on Sundays, returning home with the small van full to busting with all sorts of wonderful things.

John's mind now turned to having a house in France. He duly took off in a sort of hybrid Mini car, firstly to Ibiza to check on the villa and then meandering back looking at properties in the Dordogne. An old farmhouse needing a lot of work was spotted and an offer made. Christmas was approaching and young John was home, so a trip was made in small Fiat van with the necessary tools to begin work. It was a charming location, lovely people, but a pretty derelict house. The idea was all a bit silly as John was now suffering from angina and was quite unwell. Also he had no intention of attempting to learn the language.

'Well, let's just keep running and maybe we won't notice we are ageing!' thought Angela. John was off again south, flying this time to Ibiza, and did not tell Angela what flight he was returning on. So she did not meet him at the airport, which got a black mark. Angela went off to work as usual next day, returning home to find no sign of John, nor was he seen or heard of for months; even the police did not find a trace. Angela was pretty sure he would be in Canada but he had not contacted the family in Toronto. She felt abandonment, rejection, anguish, anger, betrayal, guilt, loss of trust – all those things and more, but there was no sign of John, till a phone call after about six months from a somewhat inebriated husband, in Canada. He'd return if wanted. What does a person say? 'Well, let's give it a go and forgive; yes, that's what to do,' thought Angela. The problem, of course, was that trust had been lost and that takes a long time to rebuild; and can one truly forgive when one has been in effect abandoned again? At that time Angela had no spiritual understanding of the need to forgive. As most women probably do, she thought it was most likely her fault and she must try harder!

John did return, but deep down the question was 'When will it happen again? Is there really much of this marriage to salvage? Is this the ten-year curse coming into effect?' Now there was another scheme; why not holiday in Ireland, the country of John's family's origin, though that was Protestant and very Orange Northern Ireland? Southern Ireland was the choice, and why not have a house built? Plot of land bought, plans and a builder sought, timeframe for building set, but did one believe the Irish blarney? Angela left her job just as she was about to be promoted to County OT, which in some ways was a wrench, as her career was really beginning to take off and she was enjoying the challenge. The hardware business and house were sold and off went the couple to pastures green in Ireland, close to Bantry Bay on a peninsular jutting out into the Atlantic – sublime! There was a garden to construct, curtains to make, the new Aga to try out, golf to play, and the finest seafood brought to the door for free.

Life chugged on at Irish pace, friends were made and golf played, there were visits from family and so on. 'Surely this is not what life is about?' thought Angela. What a waste of her career, and really where was this all going?

One day Angela was not feeling well which was unusual, but went with John to play golf, whereupon a major argument ensued. There was silence on the journey home and Angela went to bed to think. Return to Canada? This was not an entirely new thought; get a job and get on with life alone, leave John to stew in his own juice. Next day Angela took a trip to town, and bought a one-way ticket to Toronto for the following day. John was told of the plan; he knew there was nothing he could do but take Angela to the airport. He too knew in his heart that this marriage had in effect ceased to be one.

There had been discussions about Canada before but John really didn't want to go, as he would have to look for work, and he was in reality out of that loop, with his age and health. But lingering in his mind was yet another madcap idea of owning a farm. Angela, apart from being interrogated in New York about her citizenship of Canada, as she had a one-way ticket, had an easy trip and was taken in by her sister-in-law, with whom she had a good relationship. Day three, she bought a car, and day four, headed for a small town called Lindsay, to look at apartments and the neighbourhood. She called in at the Haliburton-Kawartha home care office to ask if they needed an OT. The director was out for lunch but met Angela on her return and said they had no OT programme but needed to start one.

'Please join us part-time,' the director said.

'When?' asked Angela.

'Monday.'

'OK.'

chapter six

CANADA AGAIN

So started the most exciting job. A wonderful chunk of Ontario to travel, five offices to serve and a chance to really develop a new service; real pioneering stuff. In Angela's spare time, properties with land were explored and one eventually pinpointed, and John, by remote control, sanctioned the purchase and arrived some months later. Somehow the Irish property was sold, though Ibiza was still a thorn in the flesh. The twenty-one acre farm was a laugh – the neighbours must have watched with glee the antics of two people without a clue. John went to market one day and came back with two goats, and in the morning there were four. Angela learned how to milk them and make cheese and yoghurt. Then there were the ducks, and the guinea hens that were quite uncatchable and therefore uneatable. They were, however, amazing guards, setting off into a unified screech if anyone should dare to come near the property. The hens laid and made good eating, as well as the ducks. Angela became an expert at beheading, plucking and gutting. Then came the worms – oh yes, a whole barn full of them in boxes with 'under worm heating' for the winter. This was to be the ecological wonder of the age, but actually the rats liked them rather well! In winter, going to work was fun; start the tractor, snowplough the drive, get breakfast and guess what, plough again. Sometimes the temperature would be minus thirty degrees, nose freezing and eyebrow icicles! A thousand maple trees were planted to harvest maple syrup. John chose to be away when they needed planting, a trip to Spain again, so Angela rang some friends and had a weekend planting. The maple trees by the roadside were tapped and great was the excitement of the dripping syrup until someone said little boys had added 'liquid' to the syrup! End of the maple syrup dream.

There was some movement on the sale of the villa in Ibiza so John had gone over knowing full well that at that time one could not take money out of Spain. 'Why not buy diamonds or a Mercedes or two, but don't try money?' advised Angela. But John went to the airport with wads of money and endured a night at gunpoint, having been relieved of the money and his British passport. He was released in the morning to attend court two days later. Off he went to the Canadian consul in Barcelona and an air ticket was supplied as John still somehow had his Canadian passport. A strange message had been received by Angela, who discerned the predicament correctly but was powerless to do anything. John finally returned home but a noticeable change had taken place and perhaps the term 'a broken man' would be appropriate. Shortly thereafter John took an overdose and was found unconscious by Angela, who called the ambulance and he went to hospital.

This event was again not dealt with by Angela and left a lasting wound which affected her greatly. Had Angela perhaps failed again? Could she have done more? Could she have been a better wife? Why was it she always seemed to be abandoned? Perhaps this was the final turning point in what was by then a very rocky marriage, with Angela at the peak of her career, and surging on and John well past middle age, unwell and staring into the abyss of old age. Could it be that the person that John had helped to shape and encourage and teach was turning into someone he disliked and of whom he was, in fact, jealous?

Throughout this time Angela had been finding she was seeing double and was unsteady on her feet. She thought perhaps she was in the early stages of multiple sclerosis. A visit to the doctor confirmed things were not working and eventually, after the usual tests, scans, spinal taps, evoked potentials and EEG, a diagnosis of MS was given. The only positive thing in this was Angela had a much clearer idea how the many MS patients she worked with had been treated by their neurologists – in a quite cavalier fashion which left them totally bewildered. Determined for this diagnosis not to be a fact, she kept going and through time the symptoms went away; it was probably a wrong diagnosis, and the symptoms all a huge stress issue.

Angela, having now firmly established OT in this huge area with five other OTs, was asked to move to the southern office full-time, which appeared to her as not exactly fair. However, it seemed it was more feasible for her to move than others. Eventually the farm was sold but Angela had found accommodation in a British Legion facility. She was eligible because of John's army service and his age. Frequent trips back to England took place to support the now eighty-year-old DL, who had valiantly visited almost every year, wherever the couple were. One time while Angela was away in England visiting DL, John found an advertisement for an OT post in Peace River, Alberta. The time in Ontario was coming to an end in terms of government constraints and restructuring, so Angela contacted them. She flew out and got the job on the management team of the health unit covering an area the size of Britain, which was a good promotion and pioneering again. The pair drove out in two vehicles, one a motorhome that they had owned for some time and Angela's new 4x4. It was a new and exciting job with teaching others being the only way forward in that huge area with miles between houses and acres and acres of nothing.

New territory to explore, hard town, first experience of Native Canadians, the Metee (a cross between French-Canadians and native people); their language was Cree. It was so disturbing to see first-hand what horrors alcohol, disease and ring fencing had done to these wonderful people. An example of colonialism gone mad, these

37

people were deprived of their native lands and their livelihood of hunting and fishing. They were, to all intents and purposes, put into a compound miles from anywhere and given the very basic necessities of water, housing, health care and education. Any attempt to discuss this state of affairs was met with: 'Mind your own business!'

Cross-country skiing by moonlight, bears, coyotes howling, moose and caribou; it was real frontier stuff. Minus 40 below, driving on dirt or ice roads alone for long distances daily was a challenge, and not for the faint-hearted. The winter gear kept in the car in case of breakdown was quite extensive – an axe, candles, matches, dried food, sleeping bag, and water. There were no mobile phones then, and anyway, they would have been out of range.

The couple motorhomed at weekends, exploring the vast and varied area. The Alberta soil could turn to what was known as 'gumbo' when it rained – slimy, slippery and impossible to move in. One weekend when going out for the first time in the new pick-up truck with demountable living quarters, John took a wrong turn and ended up stuck in the gumbo. The 4x4 was useless. Angela and John tried scooping out the water from the tyre tracks, to no avail. By now in bare feet and gumbo-encased bodies in the brand-new truck, they gave up for the night, and tried again in the morning. With plastic mugs the water was extracted from the channels, and some twigs and branches found to make a corrugated road. Eventually, John managed to get going and turned the truck around, with Angela waiting to jump on the back as John returned so he did not have to stop. Alas, Angela missed the jump and John, quite oblivious to this, kept going on, changing gear and getting faster, as Angela in bare feet was trying in vain to catch up. The thought of all the wild animals around encouraged Angela to move very fast indeed!

Eventually John came to safe ground at a T-junction, so he stopped to go and discuss things with Angela and get her on-board properly. To his astonishment there was no Angela! After some minutes, a panting apparition appeared rounding the bend at high speed. All she could do was to laugh and collapse in thankfulness.

chapter seven

MID-LIFE CRISIS

John got itchy feet again in 1984 and decided the winters were not for him, so he took off with the motorhome to Oregon, where he would spend the winters golfing, chatting, drinking, living an idle existence and feeling increasingly sorry for himself. In some ways this suited Angela, but it seemed a bit cruel to be grafting whilst the other half was idling time away! Job-wise Angela was enjoying life, but two things were not well – the marriage, and an ageing DL.

David had now been in the Retreat for years and was incapable of seeing to his mother in her old age, which meant that Angela felt she needed to return to Britain. There was always the feeling that she owed DL her life for having been rescued from the adoption home, a feeling of being beholden and a sense of duty. It was tough choice as she had nearly completed her OT degree and was well known and respected in OT circles in Alberta. There were TV chat shows and appearances on Canada-wide TV, talking about OT, particularly with reference to multiple sclerosis, as Angela was an advisor to the MS society country-wide. There were high-powered conferences to speak at, and a job would have been forthcoming in Edmonton or Calgary.

Next trip home to England was crunch time and Angela felt she could not orchestrate DL from afar. This would have been the time for the couple to separate, but no, John decided he would move and did so first. DL, to encourage this move, bought the couple a home. Angela went for Christmas and secured a divisional OT job in Northallerton, twelve miles from DL. The pay was appalling compared to Canada and the work ethic non-existent, but the job was good. She was in charge of six OTs and had a lovely area of North Yorkshire to travel in. Angela flew back to Britain leaving Canada on her forty-fifth birthday, making a pronouncement to a friend at the airport, 'I am going home for my mid-life crisis.' Just how true that pronouncement would become Angela had no idea, but it was the beginning of a very difficult few years. All appeared well, with a nice home in a village, DL happy, Angela enjoying work. However, John was doing nothing, barely going out, and retreating from all responsibilities, so communication between the couple was becoming less and less.

One day John announced he was going to the races in York. 'Hallelujah!' thought Angela. 'There is a spark still there.' Angela had said, 'Stay the night if you are enjoying yourself' – and doubtless having a drink or two – so she was not surprised to find that the car was not there on her return home. Picking up the mail, she spied a padded envelope with John's handwriting on it, addressed to her. Not in any way prepared for what she heard on a tape recording, Angela listened to a stream of vitriol which ended with John telling her that the car was at Teeside airport – he had taken off again with no destination mentioned.

Angela's reaction to this latest in the roller coaster ride was initially utter numbness and disbelief. Come next morning, however, there was no possibility of going to work and in fact the boss's secretary was dispatched to see what was happening. If Angela had any thought that she could get through anything, she discovered otherwise on that day. Abandonment, rejection, devastation, anger, fear, hatred, guilt, shame, failure, if there were a dictionary of emotions there would be the whole gamut. Something cracked in the depth of her being and it would be years before the healing of that day took place. Actually, Angela just suppressed most of the really deep emotion and just kept on going. The immediate action was a visit to the doctor who promptly prescribed the same drug that her brother, David, was on. This made Angela realise she must have been in a state. She took the pills for three days and decided there was a better way than drugs, which was to tough it out. 'Keep busy, suppress all the emotions, go into overdrive, and let's pretend it never happened.' Somehow that response was not a conscious decision, but a subconscious one, and there was no awareness at all of the impact this would have and the ensuing effect upon her life.

Working with Angela in the office were two fostering and adoption officers who were constantly discussing Section 22s (people who had been adopted and had applied to social services in order to begin the search for their biological parents). Angela had on her desk the form for doing this, but had not felt it right to pursue this idea with all the other turmoil going on. In fact, she had invented a story about her parents which seemed quite plausible and stopped her having to deal with the issue. The story went that Angela was conceived during the war and her father was killed and her mother died in childbirth, not an impossible idea. It saved her having to deal with other less savoury possibilities, like being abandoned and rejected – again a form of denial and fantasy.

One Thursday evening on her weekly visit to DL on the housekeeper's day off, DL asked Angela to photocopy some portion of the family tree, on which of course Angela was not included, as adopted children were not added. Next day in preparation for the following week's visit, Angela duly photocopied the material. Visiting the following Thursday she handed the copy to DL and was amazed to find herself saying how hurt she was by not being on the family tree, legally adopted but not accepted. In the next breath she asked if DL had any information on Angela's biological mother. The reply to this question was a stunning: 'No. I threw all the information out.' Angela was furious. An immediate inner response was made to fill the form in on her desk and start the quest to find her mother. It was always a hunt for mother not father, as they – fathers – did not feature in Angela's life, and inwardly she probably felt they were not safe people who could be trusted.

ANGELA NOW

chapter eight

FINDING MA

As you may have guessed, I am Angela.

A new and different phase of life started after I made the decision to find my mother before there was no longer a possibility of her being alive. The form was filled in and the director at work asked for his advice as I had to undergo counselling and did not feel the two people in my office would find it easy, nor would it be appropriate for them to counsel me. My director mentioned the name of a counsellor in Ripon whose name seemed vaguely familiar. I made an appointment to visit her amid growing excitement that this could indeed be life-changing or a disaster. The counsellor turned out to be my ex-matron from school who, of course, knew I was adopted, though it had never occurred to me that any of the staff at school would have had any idea. I think I never actually told anyone I was adopted at The Mount school, though I did initially when I was at Polam school. Was this denial? A burial of the truth?

My counsellor told me what I would need to consider before she could pursue the process, most of which I had already thought of, but of course in the event one is not prepared for at all. Questions like: How would you feel if there were siblings? How would you react if she did not want to see you? What about your father? What about illnesses? What about social status, and so on?

The only information I could supply was that I had been adopted from the National Adoption Society who had recently been taken over by Brent social services, who at that time were considered to be the most inept social services department in the country. However, they had employed the lady from the adoption society, which was a miracle. Some weeks passed and the counsellor called at my home with encouraging information. She had in her hand letters that my mother, whose name was Diana Thornton, had written shortly after my birth on 4 February 1941.

I take it that when I have heard from you that the medical report &c is passed I may apply for a vacancy at Temple Guiting. Hostel? I am so very glad to know the Committee have agreed to help & it is a great relief to me, though I very much hate parting with my baby. But I think it must be for the best really

Yours truly

Diana. M. Thornton

It is not possible to put into words what seeing that piece of paper felt like, and to hold in one's hand something that had been written by one's own flesh and blood. This can still reduce me to tears! There was more information as my father had admitted paternity, so his name was mentioned and the birth certificate gave addresses to follow up. Next stop was the local library and the phone book to look up my father's surname which was an unusual spelling of a quite common name; he had lived in the small village of Dulverton in Somerset. There were two mentions of men with that surname in the phone book so I duly gave them to my counsellor to contact. Time passed and no reply, so taking things into my own hands (again!) and against perceived wisdom I planned to go down to Somerset in person and scour the graveyards for more information. A slight hiccup happened in the person of John who had decided to return, not entirely with my approval or blessing – and yet, could this marriage be redeemed? I had to give it a go, again me thinking I could solve all things! Always in control, me on the throne of my life.

The graveyard at Morebath near Dulverton where I had expected to find Grandfather's or Grandmother's graves provided nothing. It was Harvest Festival at the church in Dulverton and ladies were decorating the church, so I enquired of them if they knew of my mother; they said not. They mentioned a man who would know, so I visited him the next day and he was most helpful. He had been a good friend of my father's, and although I did not say who I was, he gave me a look that told me that he knew. He suggested I contact my father's two sons and they would be better placed to help; no mention of my mother at this visit.

There was now a serious choice to make. 'Do I dare to continue and face the ramifications or shall I call this whole chase off?' I knew I had to do it, so phoned up one brother, John, and made an appointment to see him the next day. I did not let on who I was but that I was looking to find Diana Thornton and felt he may know where I might find her.

What does a girl wear to meet her brother? How would the visit go? So many questions and a mounting excitement! Greeted at the door of the farmhouse by John and welcomed into the parlour, we sat down and chatted but evaded the issue until I asked if he had received a letter from my counsellor, which he had. Then there was the realisation of who I was and that we were half-brother and sister. This was the first time I had ever met a blood relative. I had always despised the 'blood is thicker than water' statement!

Can one even describe what it felt like? The whole range of emotions, some of which I did not recognise, having bottled up such things for so long… Now what? 'Well, do you know where my mother is?' came out of my mouth next.

'No,' came the answer, 'but I know where her sister is, just five miles away.'

We arranged to meet later that night to meet my other brother, Gerald, and spend time together. I was not surprised to find the men had known about me for years, and so had their mother, now dead; therefore I was not going to cause too much pain to anyone. They filled me in with details of my father and drew a picture of his life for me. They had brought photos as well. Bill, my father, had died aged seventy-six in 1977 of an epileptic fit, the fits having only started in his later years.

There was still time to abort the quest, but I felt I had to continue. So next day I set off to find my aunt. She was not at home but a friendly neighbour who was a police officer gave me, against all rules of policing, my cousin's phone number and said my aunt was in her flat in London. Mobile phones were not around then, so I returned to the hotel and sat down with a whisky to pluck up courage to phone the cousin, because then this chase could not be aborted. My Canadian accent was still intact so my story sounded quite authentic. So when Sheila, my cousin, answered the phone and I posed my question there was an immediate 'Aunt Diana? Of course I know where she lives – in Inverkeilor in Scotland, and here's her phone number.'

I sensed immediately if I did not ring now, Sheila would beat me to it and all might be lost, so without pausing for a sip of scotch I dialled and enquired if the person on the other end of the phone was Diana Mary Thornton.

'Yes.'

I said, 'Are you sitting down?'

'Yes.'

'Does 4.2.41 mean anything to you?'

Without the slightest hesitation, Diana said, 'Where are you, who have you told?' I thought she sounded awfully posh and she could barely understand what I said, not being used to Canadians. We chatted and questioned each other and then Diana asked, what did I want to do? I immediately said, 'To meet you.'

We arranged that I would travel back to York and drop John off, and I would head to Scotland alone and meet her in two days' time at a hotel suggested by her. I could not visit her at home because she was a single woman and no one (not even her sister) knew about me, and of course I might look a bit like her. So began the last leg of this quest to find my mother and find answers to some of the questions which had always, from deep within, required an answer.

The night in the hotel in Edzell was a torment. I had by then spent several hours on the phone talking to Diana and it seemed she knew I was looking for my roots, as she called them, and she said when we met she would show them to me. Sleep was not a possibility as there were so many questions tumbling around my head. I phoned Diana in the morning to say I could not possibly meet her in public. Could she come up to my room? Now, what does one wear? I thought she would want to see my legs, so put on a skirt and a comfortable top. I kept looking out of the window waiting for a blue Subaru to park. Would she be punctual, or was that one of my hang-ups? What would she look like, would I even like her? That day I did have emotions, but they were all over the place – terror might have been one!

After what seemed like an eternity, the blue car parked and out from it came a sprightly white-haired lady. The waiting nearly over, I opened the door of my room and there were a pair of blue eyes which I had known all my life, and a tentative hug. I was later to discover that touch was definitely not a Diana thing, so this barest gesture was huge. In she came – 'Oh, you've got you father's legs, oh, and his nose and his eyes!' (I did not think my eyes were his; maybe she never looked at hers!)

Then a question to which there was no answer – 'Did you mind being a bastard?' I truly did not associate 'bastard' or illegitimacy with myself. Denial again. Actually 'bastard' was my favourite swear word then, so it changed the meaning in a hurry and dropped out of my vocabulary immediately! Diana presented me with a First World War bayonet, the only treasure she could part with from her limited possessions – one could think all sorts of things about that as a present! Continuing the conversation she said she had tried to abort me by drinking gin and poking with a knitting needle, but to no avail. It was not until a long time later that this statement was revisited and dealt with. She also told me that if she had kept me I would have been a battered baby.

After a while we went out and parked at Edzell Castle and she looked out of the car windscreen and told me about her life, her family. She had brought the family tree with her and books on the Thornton family. They had been evangelicals with many clergy through the generations, also Members of Parliament, bankers and governors of the Bank of England. Henry Thornton had been a substantial financier of Christ Church, Jerusalem. The family had helped in the founding of Sierra Leone for freed slaves, they were founding members of Bible societies, and supporters of evangelical activities. Henry Thornton, my great-great-great grandfather, lived at Battersea Rise where the Clapham Sect met and strategised; he and William Wilberforce were cousins. Henry Thornton in particular was known for generous philanthropy; his desire to give God the glory in everything he did was well known. He wrote a book on banking which is still referred to today. They were greatly influential in politics and evangelical circles; Henry was a close friend of William Pitt. In the recently redone book of Henry Thornton's family prayers, it is evident that the family prayed morning and evening for their descendants and generations to come. I am convinced that their prayers have brought me into the kingdom of God. I think their steadfast praying has affected the lives of so many of my family's generations. I give God the thanks and praise for them.

Henry Thornton, Angela's great, great, great grandfather, on The Thornton Family Prayers booklet cover

Diana was at great pains to talk about the Gaffer, as she called her father; she had an almost love/hate and turbulent relationship with him, although he had in the end lived with her on her farm until he died. Diana had, though, been included in all his sporting activities, and had experienced the seasonal migration of his sporting life from one place to another. His existence seems to be summed up by this article:

> His life revolved entirely around sport and agriculture. September to January, he shot partridges and pheasants on his Devon estate, as well as hunting foxes and stags. Then a pause until spring stag hunting, followed by trout fishing in Devon until the end of May, when he went North to Argyll and his stretch of the River Awe. Then to his estate Soval on the Isle of Lewis for salmon, trout and char fishing in June, July and August, then wild fowling preceded by snipe, woodcock, grouse rabbit and hare shooting. The return south started in time to be home in Devon for the autumn stag hunting.

He was mostly accompanied by Diana and his companion Miss Huldine Beamish who, it was said, was a friend of Hitler's and Diana long suspected of being a lesbian, but the issue was never aired by Diana or the Gaffer. There is no mention anywhere of any philanthropic activity; it seems he was completely self-absorbed. It is also not apparent from whence came his wealth; it was assumed he must have been bought out of his family banking ties with Thornton's Bank, which eventually was gobbled up by the Royal Bank of Scotland.

Diana told me she had a long-term relationship with my father, William Henry Hancox, although my grandmother had tried her best to end it. Bill, as she knew him, was born in Edgbaston. Bill's father had been a vet and a horse specialist, and Bill had had his father's love of horses and expertise, which was much in demand in the First World War. Diana told me of my conception in the back of

Bill's Ford van in a valley just off Exmoor, which she subsequently showed me. My grandmother had been supportive of her situation but my grandfather, who could have financed her, chose to ignore her plight; he was too busy pursuing his own interests. I found it very hard to forgive my grandfather for not supporting my mother in a tangible way.

My birth took place in a mother and baby home at Temple Guiting near Cheltenham and Grandmother and Diana took me aged six days to the Adoption Society from where DL collected me some time later. Diana said I was well when she delivered me to the home and her letters quoted earlier seem to substantiate this. At one point I asked her if she ever thought of me, and she said an emphatic 'No! How could you when you gave a baby away?' Of course, as time went on I found this statement was not true. After some time and, for me, a stiff neck from looking at her sideways, we went for a run in the car up Glen Esk, with which she was well familiar. We walked a while, and Diana talked and I listened; no time for questions, they came later. As darkness fell we headed back to Edzell and I enquired if Diana would join me for dinner, which provoked a rather surprising agreement. Diana left after dinner and I was unsure how things would progress, but the whole day had been so overwhelming somehow what might happen in the future was irrelevant.

I received an early phone call from Diana the next morning asking if I would visit her home and she would show me more family things. I was, of course, delighted to comply. I found her senior citizen council bungalow situated in the small village of Inverkeilor, with a carefully tended garden back and front and Clematis, her treasured and immaculate caravan in which she had lived for some years with two dogs and a cat. We had to decide on names. Diana had called me Gillian and felt she would like to call me by that name, which as it was really just for us was fine, and she wanted me to call her Ma which somehow she had called herself. I had to leave to drive home that day so we had to decide if we both wanted to continue the relationship. As we both wanted to, we made some tentative plans that Ma would visit me, though with the John thing not resolved I was not convinced it would work.

chapter nine

LIFE WITH TWO MOTHERS

I left later that morning and had great difficulty seeing as I could do nothing but cry; I just could not stop. I was amazed at the courage of Ma who, at very close to seventy-five, had had her world turned upside down within three days, and I had been on the trail for six months. Returning home was not easy and I knew that if this relationship was to continue it would be quite likely the last straw for the marriage. Ma and I phoned and wrote daily at length; we had forty-six years to catch up. I wrote a mini history of my life for her and she filled me in with hers. We used, surprisingly, the same funny words for things. We liked the same things, we disliked the same things, same food, same drink, same cars, same clothes, it was just extraordinary. Having an idea of family history gave me for the first time an answer to the questions of 'Any diabetes or cancer in your family?' when going to a new doctor. This blood thing was odd.

I grew to love Ma, but it was not in any way the same love I had for DL; it was a new kind of love that came from inside which I had not experienced before, although of course love for me was somewhat of an unknown quantity. Actually, Ma was not easy to love; she was an embittered, critical, rude old woman with not much pleasant to say for anyone. Underneath was this lovely, rejected, hurting, lonely lady whose dreams had been shattered and who had lived financially by sheer hard work, looking after horses, running her own small holding, landscape gardening, caring for an old man, or running a bed and breakfast. Finally at sixty she had decided to sell her home and buy a caravan named Clematis and live a nomadic life with her two dogs and a cat. One dog was always a corgi, as my three dogs had been! After a few visits, Diana asked if she could hold my hand which was a mega step for her, and thereafter for a while we both seemed to touch each other and hug and kiss, which was almost bordering on a wrong relationship. The lack of nurture on my part and the lack of nurture and love in her life somehow needed to be met. Ma took easily to being treated to good meals and some good holidays, which strengthened our relationship and provided real opportunities to get to know each other.

The relationship blossomed and visits were made by both of us to each other's homes. But underlying this wonderful new dimension to my life were two issues that needed to be resolved. One was John and the other was if and when to tell DL about Ma, knowing that she would be grievously hurt. DL was by now in a nursing home, so could I delay and maybe escape having to tell her at all? The John issue was in my face, and quite honestly I could see no way out but to ask him to leave.

Both the boys had given up on their father. They did not see why I was so soft, and in fact they encouraged me to let him go. DL, of course, would be delighted as she had never liked him. So finally he did leave, and it was with no regret nor emotion that was palpable that I watched him get into a taxi and that part of my life was over. John died some years later in Canada after we had gone through an acrimonious divorce, the divorce lawyer asking me to put on paper a hundred reasons why I wanted to divorce him. That was a cruel way to end a marriage as there had obviously been some good times, but somehow they were overshadowed by the list. In fact, I would not have divorced him had DL not said she had changed her will and I would receive nothing if I did not. That was perhaps the bottom line of manipulation, and worse, I succumbed.

I had had to make arrangements for DL to go into care the year before after a series of mini strokes which I had observed while I had been with her. She had moved, aged eighty, to a smaller home in Darlington and was still able to employ a housekeeper, a daily and a gardener, so it could have been possible for her to remain at home, and be cared for. I could have ceased working, and could therefore have moved in and orchestrated a series of carers. I knew that deep down I was not made of martyr material and that I would resent DL and the curtailment of my freedom after a few days. Part of me thought I owed it to her and part recoiled at the thought, as I had spent the best part of two weeks seeing to her needs unaided and knew my feeling could well turn to hatred within a short space of time. It was a hard decision that the doctor and I came to after a full stroke when she was rendered speechless and paralysed down one side. How hard it was to explain when she could not respond but by the anguish on her face that made me want to run away.

In fact, she made the transition to a nursing home with great grace and I placed her in a home where her housekeeper of twenty years was living as well. The next decision to be made was to think about the house, car and contents, so in conjunction with the solicitor, we decided we would put the house on the market, but of course DL had to sign. I remember so well having to ask her to sign her name, which I knew full well she could not do with her right hand. I watched helpless as she discovered she could not hold the pen, let alone write. Not daunted she put the pen in her left hand and managed a not dissimilar signature. Her bravery was a fine example to me. She began slowly to recover from her paralysis and began to walk again, to use her right hand, and her speech returned almost to normal. It was then that I was able to take her out and we rediscovered places she and I as a child had treasured. We began to enjoy each other's company without the daily strain of caring. It was a restorative and healing time for both of us.

One summer day I took DL out from the nursing home to a lovely garden called Harlow Carr at Harrogate. We borrowed an electric buggy and had a happy day, until I told her about Diana. Her reaction was typical of her – very little, just a 'long look' I knew so well, a look of pain which said it all, but nothing verbal. I thought there would be a riposte and later it came via mail, but even then it was a considered and graceful response hiding the deep pain she must have felt. We had both learned to stuff down anything remotely termed 'emotion' and put a lid on it.

Sat.

Dear Angela,

Turning things over in my mind – I realise that I have never wanted you to research your past – that I wished to forget as much as possible that you did't enter the family at Birth. To have your real Mother so suddenly produced has shaken me very badly.

I know I'm very badly

What I did not know at that time was that DL had conceived David out of wedlock, only DL managed to get Carew to marry her, unlike Ma who was unable to marry because my father, Bill, was already married. I think this is why they both respected each other and, in a strange way, became friends. The first meeting between them was initiated by DL, who I was visiting in her nursing home. She knew Ma was staying with me, in fact we were staying in DL's house and Ma was helping me sort DL's stuff out. DL asked me to bring Ma in so I went to ask Ma, who promptly burst into tears. She said she couldn't but did, whereupon DL burst into tears and I felt like a ping-pong ball. I really was struggling with all sorts of emotions with which I was incapable of dealing, but did one day go into the garden at DL's house and get all the clay pots out of the greenhouse and smash the lot against a tree - my version of anger management!

The outcome of this visit was that in a strange way, as I have said, the mothers became friends. They had similar backgrounds, both from banking families, both brought up on large estates and both privately educated. They would enquire of each other when I was visiting, and if I was abroad Diana would always phone DL to see how she was. There seemed to be little if any animosity, but the glue that kept them talking was their daughter, me.

chapter ten

IDENTITY CRISIS AND CONVERSION

With John gone, DL told about Ma and work becoming increasingly frustrating and financially unrewarding, I called time on working and retired early. My constant trips up to see Ma were making me feel that I wanted to be nearer her. DL was cared for, her house and effects all gone, David was in the Retreat, John was gone, so why not make my choice of where to live? A house was found in fact by Ma in a nice village near Perth about twenty-five miles from her. The only snag was, Ma decided to move in first which was not the intent. I had discovered rather to my amazement when I left work that I had no real identity. I was no longer a wife, a mother in the real sense, or an OT. That was quite a scary place – actually, I had no idea at all who I was. I began to formulate the possibility of starting an OT business servicing the legal profession and becoming an expert witness. In the meantime, Ma was continuing to tell me about her life and instil in me some of her passions.

Ma and I did a great excursion to Somerset with the intent of her showing me the places of her youth, her life and friends. We embarked on a journey, as two almost strangers learning to understand each other's ways. Of course it was not easy. I found the most difficult bits were when we went to see Diana's friends who knew nothing about my existence. Diana would go in to see her friends unannounced and chat a while as I sat in the car. Time would elapse and then she would emerge and take me in, the crime confessed. I felt like exhibit A. In fact I was graciously received and welcomed by everyone, even Diana's ex-fiancée who had ditched her when she had confessed my existence. We rented horses and rode over Exmoor, Diana not having ridden for twelve years. Ma who wanted to show me where she had hunted and where she and Bill had met, and where I was conceived. And we met with my brothers, who had known Diana well. That was an interesting night!

John and Gerald, my brothers, had known Diana well in their childhood as Ma had often spent time at the Lion Stables in Dulverton, which Bill rented. She would be waiting for the Gaffer to return from hunting, or waiting to hire a horse, or just plain working with the horses and the boys would be there. Evidently it was not just Diana who took Bill's eye, but Diana's sister Monica, who was the eldest of the Gaffer's second family, Diana being the youngest. Diana found the thought of meeting the brothers quite difficult, but I had been out with them before and sort of paved the way. In fact, it was an excellent meeting; some real reminiscing of old times ensued which for me was riveting.

Horses were the catalyst. Ma took me to Gleneagles to watch American Quarter Horses. I had ridden some in Canada and liked the American way of riding. Anyway, lessons were next but it became obvious it would be cheaper to buy the horse than pay Gleneagles for lessons! Ma was the expert, having looked after and ridden horses all her life. So there was a new set of people to meet and an opportunity to go to compete in Western Riding shows and do long distance riding. At one show my horse, without me on her, won a class! I got talking to a lovely American lady, Pat, who had judged my horse and asked her if she would come to teach at my place as I had bought a twenty-one acre farm. Plans were made for Pat to return later in the year which she duly did, arriving with a huge suitcase, the contents of which were all Christian, Bible, tracts, tapes and books! Oops; I did not know she was a Christian.

Ma had taken herself into a senior citizen's residence in a town about thirty miles away, which was good for both of us. Ma had found becoming a parent at the age of seventy-five quite difficult. Our similarities infuriated her and she felt trapped, having been alone all her life. I have a letter from her explaining her decision and her pain.

Of course, to me it felt like being abandoned again.

I took Pat down to Darlington as I needed to see DL and Pat was heading for London to judge shows. I had rather stupidly said as we passed by a derelict house on our journey, 'Oh that's ripe for conversion!', to which she agreed and said so was I. So on Darlington station, minus my two front teeth that had come unglued, I admitted I needed a Saviour, after Pat had explained that I was separated from God by my sin. She said that Jesus, God's Son, had come to pay the price for my sin and that I needed to give my life to him, two seconds before I put Pat on the train. She, bless her, had been insistent that I had to do it then and there. I can't say it was a Pauline experience but gradually as I read the Bible and found a church I knew I was changing and my whole outlook was too. I had found what I had been looking for all my life – love, acceptance, peace and joy – but had been looking in all the wrong places. I was sad that it had taken so long, from my early searchings that I had documented in a diary I wrote at school, going around the mountain for so many years. It took me a while to grasp the fact that Jesus, the Son of God, wanted a relationship with me and that being a Christian was not about rules and regulations and what you cannot do. It was about freedom.

Pat was a faithful mentor. She would talk with me often from Florida and invited me out for Christmas to ride horses and attend her church in Lakeland, Florida. That was an overwhelming experience, walking into what appeared to me to be a theatre with people talking in tongues – supernatural languages they had not learned, as mentioned in the New Testament! I was welcomed by the leadership and given ample opportunity to ask questions and meet socially with Pat's friends, and even able to sit in their healing school (I have to say I never witnessed any healing). I returned several times for more of the same and discipling.

As well as the riding and keeping my twenty-one acres in good shape, I was visiting DL every month, which took up four or five days, and I worked at the nursing home when I was there as a consultant. DL phoned me every night at 6.30 p.m. on the dot, so there was no escape. I had made a rod for my own back because of feeling guilty if I did not meet her every need. Somehow in all of this I started my occupational therapy business, providing a service as an expert witness to the legal profession. This entailed visiting clients all over Scotland, writing lengthy reports and appearing at Court of Sessions in Edinburgh. It was rewarding, both personal and financial, ending a career at which I excelled and which had provided great satisfaction. Even when I raised my fee to £110 per hour I kept getting more work, so it took a while to actually insist I was retiring again.

Horses were a good interlude but surely there was more to life than that. I decided eventually that I would sell most of the horses (I had imported them from Pat) and move to Edzell where I could keep my two remaining horses at a friend's place. I planned on having a house built, which took time, and which I moved into a few weeks after DL died. She had always asked me to be with her when she died, which was going to be unlikely. However, I got a call to say she was not doing well, so went down immediately. Sensing that her end was coming, I made arrangements with the funeral people in case I was not there at her death. I then arranged for David to come to see her, which he did the next day. We all knew it was not going to be long; in fact, the day after David left I thought she would die, and so did she, as she told me the next day. She had not been ready though she said she was. Now a dilemma, to stay or go home. Go! So I went and was called back three days later and was there when she died, as she had asked me to be. That was a miracle. I had driven down to find her unconscious but I knew she was hearing me although she had been deaf; hearing is the last sense to go. I talked to her and read some Scripture, and sat till I needed to go to bed upstairs in the nursing home. At precisely 6.59 I woke with the knowledge that I had to get down to DL's room without delay. So, flinging on a dressing gown I ran down and walked into her room to be greeted by four nurses with the lights blazing, just sitting there, evidently training a new nurse how to deal with dying people. I was not amused. However, I went straight up to DL and took her hand, whereupon she gave my hand an infinitesimal squeeze and departed this world with great peace. I had told her of my acceptance of Jesus and what it meant to me so she wanted to do the same. She knew of my increasing involvement with a church and maybe she witnessed a change in me.

It was some time before I realised just how much I had felt I had to do everything I could for DL. She in turn had the expectation that I could make anything happen. She was quite convinced that I would organise her every wish. It had not impacted me that actually I was controlled and manipulated by her. So, suddenly, after she died, I found a freedom I had never known, a relief from the never-ending guilt of owing my life to DL. I was fifty-eight and only just cutting the ties, not yet understanding about soul ties – which I would find out about as a Christian – but almost understanding them inside. DL's last years had been in many ways a good time for us both, and although she depended on me to solve anything, we did in the early days of her incarceration, have many good trips out. We revisited some places we had loved and reminisced about, having sometimes the kind of laughter that is about nothing but is so releasing.

The last years were a time where she was able to share some of the awful times of her life – her father dying when she was eight; her brother, who she adored, dying at the age of twenty-one in a climbing accident and she being left with her controlling, manipulating, fragile, infirm mother who died when DL was thirty-eight. She was able to talk about her fear of being courted for her money, as she had inherited a considerable sum and had an estate to manage. This in fact stunted her choice of mate and made her vulnerable. She talked about her relationship with Carew and just how it was when she realised she was pregnant, and how devastated she felt when he asked for a divorce when he was seventy. Clearly she had a fondness for him as she had two letters from him in her handbag when she died. She was actually able to share so much of her sad life as a little rich girl, with actually no real and genuine happiness and love. Carew had only married her because she was pregnant, and she was able to share just how all of that had felt and how lonely her life had been.

She was an amazing woman who would have loved a university education, but needed to be at home with her mother. So she threw herself into doing good works, and learned early on in life to look at others less fortunate than herself. She told a lovely story about being sent into the village at Christmas as a young lady to distribute the Christmas gifts to the villagers, who were mostly miners. She felt condemned by what she felt was a paltry offering and had said so to one of the recipients. The riposte was 'Nay, hinny, that will make a fine Christmas.' She had asked a miner man coming back from the coalface why he was so dirty, again the riposte 'Nay, hinny, not dirty, just coal dust.'

Apart from starting a school, she was president of the local National Council of Women, where she campaigned against tall turnstiles and the need for rear lights on bicycles. She gave a wonderful talk to the NCW on her Edwardian childhood that I have on tape. She worked at and chaired the family planning branch in Darlington for years, an attempt perhaps to prevent others from getting pregnant out of wedlock. She was also on many Quaker committees, both locally and nationally, one being called Meeting for Sufferings – I used to wonder why would anyone go to London for that. She was also a very able tennis player with the most dynamic underarm daisy-cutting serve. The outer appearance belied a timid, crushed, fragile, sad and lonely person. To me, she was an unemotional, private, daunting, superior and quite frightening mother. She would be, I think, horrified for me to say that, but she was emotionally unable to meet one's need through her own pain and sorrow; her life, which seemed privileged, had been far from easy and she was emotionally stunted.

chapter eleven

PREPARATION YEARS

The new house in Edzell was good and I found a house group nearby – a small group of Christians with whom to share the Bible and fellowship. An American pastor was anxious to plant a church locally and we met at my house for a while, so I grew in my faith – maybe not with all the right teaching, but I was connected. I was still drinking too much scotch, and smoking, and had, as many do, tried without success to quit many times. One night I had a very clear word from the Lord who said if I did not give up smoking and drinking then the job that He was preparing me for He would give to someone else. That was in the middle of the night – in the morning I got up and never had any desire to do either. I have not smoked since and did not drink for six years. My favourite drink was malt whisky. I lived near Dufftown, the Whisky Capital of the World, and couldn't stand the smell of it. I had loads of time on my hands, and what better place to walk with my two dogs, Texas Boy, the corgi and Miss Winner, the whippet cross, than up Glen Esk. It seemed like a time of preparation; for what, I had no idea.

Travel and holidays are always a difficult time on one's own. Ma was not up to much travel by now, so I bought a motorhome and began a period of travel around Scotland, staying on beaches, in forests, by rivers and lochs with time to read and study the Bible, and actually do a Bible course by correspondence. That was a really special time with no huge commitments and a chance, really, for the first time in my life to just 'be', or at least what I thought was to 'be'!

Ma was getting frail. She had asked me to go and tow her car because her battery was flat. I refused, as the thought of towing Ma around Arbroath did not seem a good idea. I phoned the garage and shortly afterwards she decided that her days of driving were over, so I ended up with her car, my own car and a motorhome. A while later, I went shopping with her and realised she was confused and needed help. This was at a time when they Ministry of Defence was selling houses on the old Edzell airbase. I was able to buy two, one for Ma and one for someone to look after her, next door. This was quite acceptable for Ma, and she moved in with delight. She thrived on being independent but having someone she knew just next door. My friend who, with her first husband had looked after me and my farm, was single at this point and willingly came to live next door and care for Ma, who she already knew well. So it proved to be a good solution for a few years.

I realised in time that Edzell was not an ideal place for me to grow old – limited shops, no bus, no train and pretty unfriendly. So maybe I should go back to York, a city I liked and also where I knew many people – and, of course, David was still there. Actually, in many ways I knew I was becoming more and more like a hermit. I was independent, secure financially, and really thought I needed no one. Should I really bite the old-age bullet and get a flat with no garden and within walking distance of the city? I set off in my motorhome to explore this idea in detail and with lots of time, so it became a sort of holiday. After some time I came up with a new-build property near the station in York, an ideal location, four minutes' walk to the city centre, with a balcony which would prevent one getting cabin fever, and a nice layout. Seemed a good idea and as it was only just in the first stages of build, it would take a year to get entry. That was alright too, so I put a deposit down and went home to sell the house.

The other issue that would need to be resolved was that of my two dogs. Clearly two was not a possibility and as Winner, the whippet cross, was a great lover of water, the proximity to the River Ouse probably meant a new plan for her. This was, in fact, resolved by one of my close friends who was missing the companionship of a dog. She knew Winner well, so she eventually went to be with Carole, a friend from house group.

It was Carole who had sent me a brochure from a Christian healing and discipleship ministry, called Ellel which was running a two-week school of prayer and intercession – my friend knew I had been drawn towards intercession. This sounded interesting, and as I had the time and the money, I applied. Little did I know just how significant an impact this application would have for the remainder of my life.

I drove my motorhome from Edzell to Kilravock Castle – at that time the current Ellel centre in Scotland – with my faithful corgi, Tex, on board. We were heading initially for a caravan park a few miles from the centre. I was to be non-residential and I had absolutely no idea what to expect, but felt somehow I was meant to be there. There seemed a lot of teachers ready to share with the delegates. The timetable looked daunting with few spare slots and lots of group times that I looked at with a bit of horror. One good thing about being on your own is you don't know anyone, and I could run away if I wanted to – my usual means of dealing with fearful situations!

As the two weeks went by, I understood just how little I knew, and that in itself was useful. I was challenged all round. Particularly challenging was the worship, and singing which so long ago I had been banned from doing. I was sure I was always out of tune until some kind worship leader in my group said no, I was just an octave lower. That really gave me the confidence to open my mouth and at the end of two weeks, my vocal cords were quite sore. I was quite astounded by the depth of the teaching, and the truth it brought. The fellowship had been quite surprising and I really had found the whole experience quite profound. At the end of the time, I had been very challenged by the account of the work of Ebenezer (Ebenezer is a Christian ministry concerned with helping Jews around the world to make *aliyah* – returning to Israel), and talked with the prayer coordinator for Ebenezer about the possibility of volunteering as an intercessor in Odessa in the Ukraine. The other challenge I felt the Lord saying was, 'What are you going to do with the rest of your life? I have a destiny for you and I want you to walk out in it.' I had a brief talk with Anna, the director at Kilravock, and suggested I may have time and could I be used in any way? Of course, I was in the middle of moving to York from a place south of Aberdeen, but that seemed irrelevant.

Towards the end of July 2002, I had sold my house, and the flat in York was not ready, so an opportunity to motorhome again was presented. I packed up and stored my stuff and set off up into Aberdeenshire to explore the coast. I had tentatively arranged to meet with Anna at some point and so phoned to set a time. I can remember with great clarity the meeting, and the outcome was a very gracious acceptance that I might have some input into the ministry – doing what, I did not enquire, hoping it would not be money or office work. I wondered why Anna had thought with no ministry experience nor understanding of Ellel, and getting on in years, I could be of much help. We decided I should come on a healing retreat sometime soon, which turned out to be November. My application for Ebenezer had been successful and I would be needed in March of 2003. Anna agreed that I could start when I returned in late May 2003.

The healing retreat came and went without too much deep stuff being looked at – in fact, my counsellor seemed to think I was quite well put together! The second counsellor has since told me she thought I was very controlled and gave a good impression, but what she saw was not the real me. How right she was. Maybe I was a good actress. So now it was time to move to York and settle in and prepare for the Ukraine. I was surprised when I received an invitation for the Ellel Prayer Conference, which would finish just before I left for the Ukraine. That was another challenge, as most of the people were familiar with the ministry and all its centres and courses and leaders, and I was not. It was a real delight to meet with so many varied people who really had the ministry and its vision in their hearts. The ministry had only just moved to Blairmore House and this was the first event, the team trying valiantly to find out how everything worked. I was more excited than ever at the prospect of joining the team, even though Anna had mentioned something about administration which to me could mean office and money.

Fig 1. Smelt House

Fig 2. Smelt House, side view

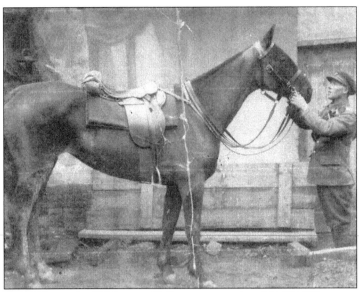

Fig 3. Bill Hancox, Angela's father, served in the war as a remount specialist 1914-1918

Fig 4. Bill Hancox, Angela's father

Fig 5. Grandfather Thornton

Fig 6. Gerald Hancox, Angela's half brother

Fig 7. Angela's father

Fig 8. Angela's father (left) and uncle Ronnie

Fig 9. Diana Thornton

Fig 10. Diana Thornton in land army uniform, 1940

81

Fig 11. Edward Carew-Shaw, 1939

Fig 12. Doris Lucy, Smelt House

Fig 13. My father, Bill Hancox

Fig 14. DL holding David and newly arrived Angela

Fig 15. Diana Thornton, 1940   Fig 16. Angela, age 3, at Smelt House, 1944

Fig 17. Grandfather Hancox   Fig 18. Angela, age 13

Fig 19. Angela and David   Fig 20. Angela and David, 1947

Fig 21. David and Angela

Fig 22. Llandudno Pier, Easter holidays, 1951

Fig 23. Llandudno Pier, 1949

Fig 24. DL, David, Angela and nanny, Frinton on Sea

Fig 25. Angela on a roundabout, Canada

Fig 26. Diana Thornton, 1987

Fig 27. Angela, age 21

Fig 28. Angela and Doris Lucy, her adoptive mother, 1986

87

Fig 29. Angela, Oxford (about 1960)

Fig 30. Angela and husband John

Fig 31. Angela's husband, John with two sons from his late wife: Peter (left) and John (right)

Fig 32. Angela, Quarter Horse Show, 1991

Fig 33. Doris Lucy's 90th birthday   Fig 34. Diana Thornton

chapter twelve

UKRAINE AND BEYOND

The journey to the Ukraine in March was uneventful, but the arrival a little panicky. I had met others on the plane who were also joining Ebenezer, so I was not alone. However, no one had shown up to meet us and we did not have an address or even a phone number, so we had to phone Ebenezer in Bournemouth. We were eventually picked up and driven to the base through what one can only describe as derelict and devastated streets. One could see the decayed splendour of the communist days all around, but the first image was of dereliction. The people appeared bent and almost expressionless, barely even alive, and one could sense the hopelessness, despair, fear and deprivation.

The base, which was very close to the Black Sea, was not really functional at that point, so we were allocated temporary rooms. I was with a lady who I had met at Ellel, so we roomed together. There were no phones or any connection with the outside world initially, apart from a few people's mobile phones. My room-mate had one which became a major irritation for me! The welcome by the team pastors was soothing, and afterwards we began to unpack and find our bearings. The dining room was about a 100-metre walk away in the grounds, and unheated. Minus 40 degrees below zero meant cold food and a cold bottom unless one cuddled one's Bible in one's coat on the way there and then sat on it, which gave a modicum of warmth. The food was perfectly edible but not what one was used to. Trips to the local shop for a Kit-Kat or even an ice cream were highlights of the week.

The whole time I was there, because the base was not really functional, and the communication issue was not fully resolved, the team could not be sent out into the wider world to find Jewish people and talk to them about *aliyah* (the return of the Jewish people to Israel). There was a sense of frustration for them, but as intercessors we did not have that problem. There were two Americans and two Britons on the intercessory team and our prayer place was one of our bedrooms. These were only twelve foot by six foot with a tiny separate en suite that consisted of a loo, basin, shower tray and hosepipe for a shower. There was a tiny balcony which was only of use come warmer weather and always looked like it might detach itself from the building. Thankfully there was heat most of the time. My room-mate had been out as an intercessor the previous year, and the same pastors were on the team. She was not up for change, nor did she respect the pastors, which was not helpful. The close quarters in the room had interesting challenges; one of mine was that my room-mate dried her hair each morning, which in itself was fine, but the smell was crematoria-like. This began to make me feel quite sick and I would dread the daily smell.

Our days began initially with breakfast in a tiny room in the main building followed by worship, maybe teaching, and an update on the day's events. Then we spent the rest of the morning praying, but as the teams were not out and about, we did not have daily requests for prayer. The real and positive benefit from my time there was the familiarity that came from reading and praying out God's word concerning Israel. After lunch we usually went exploring, often down on the beach by the Black Sea which was close by. It was very cold by any standards for the first few weeks, and even the edges of the sea were frozen. It was good to be out, though, but not really safe to go out alone. There was a strange sense of a crushing of people and a sense of espionage pervading everywhere – people were jumpy and clearly not wishing to make eye contact.

The early part of the time was particularly difficult as my room-mate hurt her back and was confined to our room and bed for several weeks. This meant me having to walk up with her meals from the kitchen twice a day. This, of course, meant I was never in the room alone, which for a single person held its own challenges The other strange thing that happened was one of the full-time Ebenezer staff was marrying a man from Ghana, who was also on staff. In fact they had had the civil wedding in England a week earlier and the Odessa team were doing the church ceremony and Ukrainian reception. For reasons I knew not, I woke up in the night before the wedding and began to cry with a sobbing I had never known before and I could not stop. It was clear that I was in no state to go to the wedding, so one of the Americans was detailed to stay with me. Eventually, by about midday, I had stopped howling and managed to go out for a short walk. I have not ever really understood what that was all about.

One weekend, Marsha from the intercessory team and I decided we would go down to Odessa and find the restaurant where the pastors and those in the know went at weekends. So began what was quite an unscheduled adventure.

It is always easy to get to the centre of a city because all the buses go there, and we had instructions. Not daunted, and excited to be getting out, we bussed down town but actually got off too soon, so we had quite a walk, and were never quite sure we were heading in the right direction. Finally we came across shops the like of which we had not seen – modern, flashy and European. We bought a few necessities and then found the eatery. What a treat – proper food, so we tarried quite a long time before we thought about the return journey. Now came the fun. We got on a bus from the opposite side of the road to where we had disembarked some hours earlier. This bus promptly went about half a mile and that was its terminus. So out we got with no idea of where we were or, in fact, where we were going, as we did not have an address of where we were staying; nor were the phones working. The added complication was one couldn't even begin to read the language, nor does French or Spanish have any resemblance to the Ukrainian language or alphabet. I am quite good at sign language and Pigeon anything, but that was no use. The only hope was that someone would speak English, but even then we did not know where we needed to go. By some miracle, a young university student was passing and saw our plight. So he joined us and eventually walked us a long way to the correct bus and got on board and travelled with us to our destination. I think he was an angel. The day out made a good story with a happy ending, which could well have been otherwise.

Time elapsed and the routine went on until the top brass of Ebenezer came out to go on the first sailing to Haifa. Then we were joined in our intercessions by the prayer coordinator for Ebenezer and the Board. We went out with the team all over the city praying over strategic locations, which was my first taste of spiritual warfare. Somehow during this time I became quite ill with an intermittent very severe pain in my stomach, which was incapacitating. This continued for several days until I thought I needed to see a doctor. Not keen at the idea of maybe being hospitalised, nor of doctors sharpening their scalpels in anticipation of extracting an organ, I asked if I could return home. This was not greeted with much enthusiasm by the Ebenezer hierarchy and the pastors; however, it was clear I was not getting better. Reluctantly, I was allowed to arrange a flight home and was taken to the airport, and even then they asked if I was running away. I was very disappointed not to finish my time there, as I was due to go on a sailing to Haifa and was going to miss my trip to Israel and a chance to really see and be with some Olim (Jewish people returning to Israel) and to set foot in the Holy Land. The flight home was uneventful, thankfully.

On getting back to York I saw the doctor, the outcome of which was that I had passed a kidney stone. I can say I never want to do that again.

That adventure and experience over, I made a phone call to Anna at Blairmore to say I would be available sooner than expected. This was greeted with some excitement as the current administrator was leaving, and if I could get there a few days before he left, he could give me some training. So plans were made to shut up the flat in York and head up to Huntly to pick up my trusted friend, my corgi, Tex. He had been living next door to Ma with the housekeeper while I was away. Not knowing when I might return it was difficult to pack, so I jammed as much as I could into my car and set off.

'Administrator,' I thought as I drove. 'That probably means money and dealing with paper and a computer.'

My computer skills were rudimentary, used only for writing long reports for my business, but not a lot else, and other people's money was going to be a challenge. David and DL used to tease me because I did not know how many pennies there were in sixpence. The more they teased me the more upset I would get – it was always at mealtimes, so I would end up under the table, crying. These episodes did nothing for my maths skills and perpetuated into senior school where I did not even attempt O-level maths. (There is a joke at Blairmore that Angela does not know how many noughts there are in 1,000. Very recently I confronted David with this teasing, and he was gracious enough to say he was sorry.

My predecessor was very patient and had made a whole manual on all the procedures that needed doing, and where to find things in the computer; all easy when he was there! Coming into that job without any background knowledge of the ministry and what it did and who was who was quite difficult. Anna was just so patient, but was not much more skilled on a computer than I, so we had a good few laughs and a few disasters. I did manage throughout my time doing the bookings not to put two women or two men in the double-bedded room. Thankfully, as I had been promised, a new team member arrived with all her skills; she could help me, though she must have been so frustrated, as was I so often. After three years in the office it was time to move on. I am sure the office people breathed a sigh of relief. It had been the best possible way of learning about the work of Ellel, meeting the numerous people from other centres who came to Blairmore. It enabled daily contact either in person or on the phone – in fact, for a while I was the voice of Blairmore for people who were making an initial enquiry. Without that experience, I would have been the poorer and it would have taken longer to understand and take on board the vision for the ministry and particularly for Blairmore. Reaching the age of sixty-five, I went part-time and had a wonderful job arranging the flowers, caring for the antiques and helping the young people to understand the importance and techniques of how to look after the furniture and treasures. I was truly blessed by these jobs, and quite surprised to be told how the flowers blessed and ministered to so many people.

One day I had, unusually for me, picked some yellow flowers for the conference hall, yellow being a long way from my favourite colour. I had felt I must pick them and, muttering away, I did so. Later that day, one of the guests found me to say that yellow was her favourite colour and she had been so blessed by the yellow arrangement. I was astounded, and from then on really asked the Lord to choose the colours and the arrangements. He was faithful in this and there were countless occasions when I was told how blessed people had been. God really is in the detail.

chapter thirteen

BEGINNING THE HEALING PROCESS

My serious walk towards healing began in November 2002 when I attended a healing retreat with Ellel Ministries at Kilravock Castle. I had come up from York with my corgi dog and wondered what to expect. I don't remember being nervous, I think I was just aware that with my adoption and being brought up in a single-parent family, there would probably be some issues arising. These were what I believed were the most damaging aspects of my life. The teaching was new to me and made so much sense. Forgiveness, acceptance and belonging, soul ties – that is, spiritual ties that bind us to another person. These can be ungodly, causing all sorts of problems. This all caused me to think deeply and challenged my understanding. The body, soul and spirit teaching was a revelation, and the reality of sin made me realise it is so rarely taught or mentioned anywhere these days. As I looked around it seemed to me that everyone else who had come looked so worn out and sad and that I was only attending because I was joining the team. In hindsight, my pride was so huge and my coping skills and acting ability were so well honed over many years that I thought I didn't have any problems!

The ministry time on the healing retreat was spent mainly with me giving an account of my life which I did without any emotion or feeling. Now, on recollection, I think a lot of my recounting centred on David, as I was not wanting to let anyone near my issues, which I had buried deeply. I remember feeling relieved at having spoken it out to people who seemed to understand and were non-judgemental. This was the very beginning of a journey, but at this point I had no idea where it was going.

As I have mentioned, I arrived at Blairmore House, the new home of Ellel Scotland, in May 2003 as a volunteer to help the very small team. As I quite clearly thought I wanted to minister to people, I decided to enrol on the Modular School as this was the foundational course that would set me in that direction. The first few courses came and went with no significant impact on me that I was aware of; my mind was set on just the training aspect of the course. I had yet to have any understanding of the damage that I had suffered throughout my life from the many times of rejection and abandonment, plus, of course, my own wrong and ungodly decisions and my sin. I was so arrogant as to think everyone else had the problems, not me. Oh, how wrong I was.

The next part of the school, in May 2004, was coming up, and I approached it unaware that God was beginning to touch some deep and buried places in my heart. The teaching on parenting presented me with a choice. Was I going to let Jesus into the buried place and let Him expose what was deeply protected inside? Was I ready to look at my coping mechanisms, my hurt, pain, anger? Actually, I said I quite liked myself the way I was, so why change and go through what I could see ahead would be a really deep surgery? I went to bed that night with a picture of a bridge over a very deep gorge, but the bridge did not meet in the middle and the gorge was too wide to jump. I woke up the next morning with this picture vividly before me, but this time I could see Jesus, on the other side of the bridge, waiting for me to go to Him. I was still not ready or able to get across to Jesus and give up my old and sinful ways. I struggled throughout the day and did not hear very much of the teaching, and by night-time I was still distressed and not ready to make the choice to give up my old ways of self-protection. I cried myself to sleep, but at some point in the night I was very aware of the Lord's presence. He showed me that it was safe to trust Him and He would help me with all my hurt and pain. At that point I gave up fighting and handed over control, and it was as if the bridge was complete and I could walk across. That was really the beginning of a new life, though there was much more to deal with.

The two Modular Schools and a couple of personal appointments were preparation time and laying foundational truths which would be built on as time went on. I came to understand that Jesus had always been with me even as a tiny baby in an adoption home, where I had lain abandoned and lonely and wanting to die, pining for my mother and growing weaker by the day. As I faced the reality of that time, I began to feel the excruciating pain of abandonment and despair which had for so long been denied. In this place of painful truth, I realised just why I needed to forgive my mother. Understanding her predicament, her desire to do the best thing for me, and her own pain at leaving me did not change the fact that this to me was a major rejection. I forgave my mother for giving me away when I really wanted her to keep me, and I also forgave my father for not taking any responsibility for me. I then forgave my grandfather for not supporting my mother, which would have allowed us to stay together. Working through forgiveness and releasing them from my judgement was pivotal in the healing process and opened the way for Jesus to bring His comfort to those deep wounds. I was beginning to realise that I did not understand pain any more than I understood the meaning of love. I thought I was living in reality but somehow the link was beginning to filter through that my fierce independence was actually a cover-up and that just perhaps I was a quite damaged.

One day my safe at home had become impossible to unlock and I tried everything I could but it still proved quite impossible to open. I knew a man who was familiar with locks and even he was unable to open it. So armed with an axe he began a radical solution, which achieved the desired result of getting to the contents. The next day I arranged for it to be collected and be scrapped. When it was finally lifted up and put onto the truck it seemed as though something of a release happened inside me. It was as if I had had a steel case inside me which I had kept locked all these years, and it was now opened and vulnerable, and more importantly, gave access to the Lord for healing. I still have the lock, which I keep as a reminder of the day when I was able to open up and allow God to work in me.

As I did this, it was becoming apparent that although I had been brought up in a privileged environment and never appeared to want for anything, I had actually been deprived of love. This was a shock to me as I saw how I had built my wall of protection so as not to look at reality and avoid the pain of the longing for love.

I began to realise I had no understanding of the real meaning of love around the time of the first Christmas when the team at Blairmore bought a small gift for each other and we had a meal and then opened presents. I found this quite horrendous and only wanted to run away; anything but having to receive or see love visibly demonstrated. To me this whole season was one to be ignored and survived. On top of that Anna and her husband, Malcolm, had asked me to join them and their boys at Blairmore for Christmas. Never having seen a Christian family experiencing Christmas I had no idea what to expect and wondered how I would survive and how soon I could escape. Helping to cook the turkey was the easy bit. That was me in 'doing mode', but the presents and fun stuff and repartee was hard. When I received a teddy bear from Anna and Malcolm, the first I had ever had, I was very emotional. Watching a family behaving as family and enjoying everything was a whole new ball game for me. Maybe I had been deprived!

As time went on, more issues surfaced; forgiveness issues, repentance issues and some anger which I realised I had always buried far down. One day I went outside with a whole roll of big bubble wrap and burst the whole lot against a tree with huge shotgun sound effects. It felt really good. I was beginning to be able to go to God myself now and ask about things, and as He revealed my sin issues and ungodly responses, I was able to take them to Him and repent. There were days of highs and lows, but there were always people around to pray and encourage and, dare I say, love me. The Father heart of God was slowly becoming a reality.

chapter fourteen

ORPHANED AGAIN

In January 2004, I was called back urgently from York where I had gone for New Year. My mother, Diana, had been taken to Dundee hospital after a very short illness which had occurred on New Year's Day. I arrived at about 6 a.m., having left York immediately after the call to see Ma hooked up to every tube imaginable and clearly not expected to live. However, a determined lady, she fought through and against all odds went back to the nursing home in Edzell. The following February, without warning, she became very ill again and when I was phoned we were in the middle of a huge snowstorm and it was late at night so I did not think it wise to set out then. There was another call early to say get there, so I set off in a snowstorm on icy roads. Just near Aberdeen Airport in a traffic jam, I was told she had died. I phoned Blairmore and Anna said, 'Come back and we will go with you.' I said to myself, 'Why would anyone do that?' I kept going and went to see Ma, and say farewell, and make arrangements.

It was so sudden and I felt abandoned all over again, and sad I had not seen her. She had given her life, although perhaps grudgingly, to the Lord a year or so back, but I was never quite sure of the reality of Jesus in her life. Some friends as well as my cousin Sheila from came to the funeral, and Anna and Malcolm and other team members came as well. I had a hard time understanding why anyone would go to a funeral of someone they did not know, but it did dawn on me slowly that they cared about and loved me.

Ma had always had a fondness for Oystercatcher birds – their call always annoyed me, so what did I see as I got out of the car at the crematorium but two Oystercatchers circling right over the chimney making Oystercatching noises! My cousin and I had a laugh. So began this slow drip feed of being able to accept love, but it was tough; perhaps the iceberg was thawing. I also made a statement that day that I would not use the name Gillian any more and would be known as Angela; the two-name thing had become like a division to my identity.

I was so blessed that I had had the chance to meet my mother and get to know and love her. It had been hard for her to become a parent all over again at her age; it was a long gap from age twenty-eight when she gave birth to me. I am always amazed at how open she was in sharing her life with me, warts and all. Whether she had always longed to see me again is a question I don't think we tackled, but her early letters would indicate she might have wanted to. She could so well have put the phone down when I first rang, and that would have deprived both of us of a relationship that was not easy but was a real joy for me. Ma changed too, and mellowed into a gentle and loving old lady with a sense of fun. She was well-liked in the nursing home and ceased to be the rude, rather tyrannical, eccentric woman I had first encountered. In fact, my cousin Sheila often comments on how much Ma changed for the better after we met. I have found it interesting to re-read her letters to me and mine to her. My nomadic lifestyle and hers were quite alike – our constant running and fear of any long-term relationship, an unreal existence, and for Ma, a very solitary one where she retreated into herself like a tortoise, almost, and which I was in danger of doing too, before Ellel.

The death of Ma after having only known her for seventeen years was a great sadness to me. My life had been so enriched by knowing her, as I think her life had been too. It was not easy to become a parent so late in life, to be confronted with traits in one's own life that one was not thrilled about. There was much of her life that she was so willing to share so openly; she really seemed to understand in a profound way my need for roots, in a way I perhaps had not grasped. There were questions I did not ask that would have been helpful in understanding some issues in my ministry times, but just having found her was alone worth everything, and I was so blessed by the way she was so open. It is a sadness that I did not meet my father, but that would have been a much more complicated procedure.

My cousin Sheila and I were to scatter Ma's ashes on the Isle of Lewis, where our grandfather had owned the Soval estate and where Diana had spent many of her holidays in her youth, fishing and walking; she knew and loved all of the island. Her father had left Soval to her and her brother, Dick, but they were unable to finance it, which saddened me. Ma would have so loved to spend her days there, and I would have also enjoyed its experience. Ma had chosen the spot on which she wished to be scattered and had showed it to me on our visit to the island a few years previously. We had met my grandfather's factor's son, Findley, who knew Ma well, and he was instructed as to the exact spot for the scatter. I had driven up to Ullapool and crossed by ferry and Sheila flew up. We met with Findley McIver and his son at the appointed place in a gale-force wind and torrential rain. Findley went up on his son's all-terrain vehicle and Sheila and I walked up the steep incline. There were few words to be said, but thanksgiving for Ma's life and an appreciation of her acceptance of me into her life in her old age. Sheila had not been to Lewis before, so we made an event of it and drove around most of the island and some of the Isle of Harris, calling in on Katie Campbell, who I had met at Blairmore, in her weaving shed. She immediately in true island style brought forth a wonderful lunch, saying, 'I wondered why I had bought this salmon and now I know.' Sheila was quite touched by the setting and the welcome. Somehow it was a fitting end to Ma's life.

chapter fifteen

HEALING: THE CHALLENGE

By this time I had a greater understanding of much of the basic Ellel teaching, but much was still in my head or sometimes not even there! There was teaching on miscarriages and the effects on people, which can be very long-lived and unresolved. I had not really dealt with my miscarriage in any godly way; it happened before I was a Christian, so I just kept going – what else was there to do? But this teaching was touching something deep inside. I had not forgiven myself for getting out and going for a walk, I had flushed a foetus down the loo without any ceremony or committal, and I had not thought about it for years. In a time of prayer ministry I was able to bring this before the Lord and know comfort and healing from much guilt and shame and the grief of loss. Jesus showed me during this time to understand that my baby had been a boy, and I was able to give him to Jesus and more amazingly, to name him Daniel. That was the name God gave me for him. That was a profound and really deeply healing time. Now I can think of him and know that sometime I will meet him, and there is no need to be hard on myself and wear the blame. The wonder of what Jesus accomplished on the cross is becoming more precious by the day on this healing journey.

As I became able to participate on the ministry team, I was continuing to understand and learn and be aware just how early on in life damage can happen. This, of course, gave me a greater perspective on the likely causes of some of my many coping mechanisms which I had developed throughout my life. They were so well entrenched that I thought they were alright. Through time I had come to realise that actually I did not know who I was, and I had invented so much of me to prevent anyone, including myself, from seeing the true me. This, of course, had put a huge barrier up between God and me which had made it impossible for Him to heal the wounds. I was now in the process of dismantling this huge defensive barrier and allowing God into the core of my being.

One of the big lessons I learned was the beginning of how to receive. I could do the giving in my own way with my time and talents, and as I had always been blessed with financial security that was quite easy. It was this receiving thing; I did not want anyone close to me who might perhaps make demands on me, or rock my carefully planned existence or, in fact, challenge me in any way. All this was dramatically altered and frightfully difficult when my beloved corgi died. He had very suddenly become very ill and the vets had no idea why; he could not and would not take the pills and was unable to eat. As a faithful and treasured companion I had to decide what was best. Anna had said not to go to the vet alone; she would come. I thought, 'Why would anyone do that? I can just take him to the vet and dig a hole in the walled garden at Blairmore and that will be it.' Anna was insistent, so not being able to fully take this love on board, I did a compromise and took him to the vet and then called at Anna's soon after on Malcolm and Anna's precious day off. Without hesitation they got themselves together and out we went to Blairmore. Malcolm, joined by another team member, dug the hole and we put Tex into it, and then repaired to the team's cottage for a cup of tea. I could not see why people would do that. I was to learn slowly – some would say very slowly – over time.

This new sense of belonging and being part of a family within Ellel Ministries, and on a more personal level with Anna and her family, was a very difficult one to grasp. There was always an attempt to rubbish the idea and run away, and be independent. Why would anyone like me for myself, not for what I could do or provide? This felt, initially, a very unsafe place to be. There were moments of almost panic and feeling trapped, but I knew that Blairmore was where I was to be and that it was safe. It was alright to be vulnerable and maybe actually say how I felt, not to always say 'I am fine' when I was like a coiled spring inside about to burst, and with a war going on in my head. There was a latent anger in me which I had never acknowledged, I had probably buried it when at Oxford for a reason I have long since forgotten. I took a pair of scissors towards a friend's chest with the definite intent of harming her. I was so appalled that I could even think of doing this that I remember thinking I must never ever let anger surface again, a vow that lasted many, many years. So, there it was; a great untapped suppressed anger which I would not admit; I was too frightened of the results of letting it go, so it lay dormant within me.

The war going on in my head gradually decreased but it seemed it may be associated with my poor memory, which had always been a trial, and was it perhaps also a result of several head injuries sustained through life? The positive side of a poor memory in ministry is that one cannot remember any formula, if there was such a thing, nor rely on remembering how others had responded. Nor could one in effect remember a lot of the teaching, one had to rely solely on the Holy Spirit, to bring to remembrance all the teaching and pointers. Also, of course, it made ministering to people very challenging as there was not a lot in the memory to fall back on.

I was very privileged to be invited to the Advanced School as a result of having completed the Modular School. It was an intensive and challenging two weeks, with numerous teachings that were not normally heard or ones that were being pioneered or refined. One such topic was dissociation – prior to that topic we had a quite rapid-fire introduction to fragmentation, which had been taught for a while. It was during worship over these two weeks that I began to feel slightly unsteady and leant against the mantelpiece which I was standing beside. I gave this no thought and put it down to being a bit tired. I was very interested in the dissociation teaching and began to think there was a distinct possibility that it had relevance in my own life. In hindsight it seems that the teaching on dissociation was stirring something in the core of my being. However, we galloped on to other subjects and there was no time to pursue the thought.

On my return home, having picked up a new car in York, I was to be on the ministry team for a healing retreat. During a lunch break I mentioned to one of the ministry team that if there was a chance, could they give me a short time of ministry? This he and Anna agreed to. I began by saying I wanted to look at some of my head injuries sustained during my life. The first one I was aware of was a car accident when I was five; the car my mother was driving with a nanny in the front and David and I in the back was struck only yards from home and we rolled over several times and were finally taken out of the sunroof. Our mother and nanny were hospitalised and David and I were taken to the aged aunt who lived next door to us. I certainly do not remember any injury, but in remembering the incident there was a sense of panic in that our mother was taken away, and it probably would have tapped into my old abandonment as a baby issue. I can remember thinking DL must have died and no one was going to tell me.

chapter sixteen

THE HEAD BANG

On the Thursday night after the healing retreat had finished, I did some shopping on the way home. I was feeling quite tired from the effects of the Advanced School, and driving home in a new car, plus almost immediately being on a retreat, not that I was leading, but just the intensity of any of the retreats. I remember going to bed about 9 p.m., and as far as I know went sound asleep. The next thing I recall is waking up lying on my back in bed, and putting my hand to the back of my head, where I felt dampness which I immediately recognised as blood. I got out of bed and went to the bathroom, whereupon I saw an Artesian Well of blood coming out of my head. Seemingly not panicked I got the phone and rang Anna, saying, 'I do not know what has happened, but there is blood everywhere.' I then unlocked the door and waited on the loo for Anna to come. She phoned 999 and the ambulance arrived speedily. They were unable to staunch the bleeding, so off to Huntly hospital I went. They could not stop it either. So I went to Elgin, a forty-minute journey by ambulance. Anna went home and made some prayer requests and asked Malcolm to come to Elgin with her. Six stitches later, hot air blankets and after varying tests, I was allowed up to the ward at 4.30 a.m. Remarkably, I was not frightened at any stage throughout this episode, and this can only have been the Lord and His comfort.

The 18 October 2007 was a day which began a real rattling in my life, not only in a physical sense but a very profound spiritual and ongoing way. Having found myself in a situation of some danger, but with no fear, I was able with great clarity to summon help, and that can surely only be the protection of the Lord. The resulting journey to Elgin hospital with blue lights flashing and the procedures which took place were challenging but manageable without pain medication, and with the support of Anna, whose hand I was able to squeeze throughout; I also had the knowledge that people were praying for me.

After about two hours sleep, I was woken and told I would be helped out of bed to eat breakfast, which did not prove to be a good idea, because I vomited; then the indignity of the commode with help, then crawl back to bed where I needed to be. For some eight hours with constant checks on me and an X-ray, I was able to make some sense of the previous night. I realised that here I was without clothes, glasses, toothbrush, money, phone, and with no means of escape. And I could do nothing about it! I had no responsibility to do anything or organise anything or say anything to anyone, a quite freeing experience. So how could this opportunity be used, and what could I learn from it? Firstly, I realised that Jesus was there and had been and would continue to be, and the overwhelming sense that people were praying for me, which in a real and tangible way I was acutely aware of. Then the realisation of just how much I had taken my health, vitality and physical abilities and mental acuity for granted. I had a really good time praising the Lord and giving thanks for all these things.

I was so comforted throughout those hours until Malcolm and Anna arrived. It was as if Jesus was holding me still and comforting me, He was ministering His love and the knowledge that I was not alone, but He allowed me to accept the situation I was in and relish the precious time I had to be still. I can assure you the sight of Malcolm and Anna was wonderful, though Malcolm's face was one of astonishment. He had not seen me the night before with my full punk rocker hairstyle of coagulated blood – I was still like that, with blood everywhere. I did not see what I looked like till later! To be reunited with some clothes and washing stuff and glasses and with some hope of escape the next day was sufficient for the moment.

Anna phoned next morning and I was allowed to go to the phone at my usual high speed – everyone was saying 'Slow down!' and Anna could hear that on the phone. Plans had been made for me to be picked up and a rota set up for people to stay the night with me, as that was the condition I was allowed to come out on. I was also not to drive for six days. I returned home to find the 'A' team had cleaned the whole bloody mess up. My bed was remade, my clothes washed and no trace of the episode was visible. They had all called my life back from the blood that had been spilt, and one of the team was waiting to spend the night. I thought, 'Is this what family is really about?'

Really good sleep followed, and then a shower – Ma always said getting up was such hard work and for the first time I agreed with her; I had had it. The next few days were filled, it seems, with people, flowers and phone calls, and I did nothing but recline, reflect and just 'be'. No gardening, no outings and no stamina to do anything but to reflect on so much that had been, on life choices, good and bad, but most of all, on the glorious truth of salvation and kingdom life and the great privilege of being just where I was at this time.

As the days went by and friends come in and out, I was still very conscious of being upheld in prayer and being in a safe place. There was growing awareness of the magnitude and omnipresence of the Lord; rather than it being a head thing, it was tangible. I could at last really grasp the Holy Spirit truly was my comforter. He will uphold you and wipe away your tears.

As time went on, I realised my body was hurting and so visited a medic who diagnosed two cracked ribs, a whiplash and a strain of my lower back (no one, including me, has any idea what happened or on what I hit my head or how I got back to bed), and advised more reclining on the sofa and pacing myself. So just watching from the safety of my home, the glorious golden days of late autumn drifted by. I had no sense of urgency to be out in the garden tidying up, no drivenness and a wonderful sense of peace – I was in 'just be' mode. How often had I heard people say 'just be' and I had thought, 'How?'

I had a meeting in Aberdeen to redo my will! So I took the train. I had time to spare in Aberdeen before my appointment. By the time I had to get a taxi I was very tired, so much so that I could barely get into the taxi and could only do so by kneeling on the floor and then heaving myself onto the seat. I had had no idea I was that weak. The return taxi man thankfully put out a step for me, but I was a bit shattered about my loss of stamina. The next challenge was that I had to phone the DVLA medical department to tell them that I had had a head injury and ask if I was allowed to drive. I phoned the DVLA on my return and was told it was alright for me to drive, so I thanked God and stopped trying to plan how I would live without a car. I had just bought a new one the week before the event. I always knew that nice cars and driving were to some degree an idol – actually, to be truthful, my car *was* an idol. I could not imagine having to ask for help and be dependent on others. The Lord really was exposing what was in my heart!

The effects of the head injury continued to limit my physical activities and I had reduced stamina for many months. I was gradually returning to work, but in a limited capacity.

It seemed that the journey back to my early years and the process of adoption was stirring deep pain and distress and reaching a place inside of me that I had never acknowledged before. I needed to allow the Lord to help me to own this place and all the pain and loneliness and anger that appeared to be there. It all appeared to start with the memory of telling my brother David I was adopted. Then the journey began as I allowed the Lord to show me the truth of how this had really affected me, rather than how I had perceived it had affected me. Actually, I had always believed it had not affected me at all! I had been living from the place of believing I should be very grateful for my adoption and work hard to justify my existence and to prove that I was of some worth.

As the Lord began to show me the truth of my real feelings and reactions, it was a very big surprise, and yet I knew it was right. I began to connect back to a place that I had abandoned years ago. With that connection came the intense pain and distress which had been covered over and denied all my life. I was aware that somewhere in my core I just wanted to die, so desperate was the sense of abandonment by my mother. There was no hope in this place; where was she? 'I am all alone, no one wants me. I am a nuisance. I want to die.'

As the Lord showed me this abandoned baby that was really me, I began to feel a strange sense of compassion and a desire to reach her and comfort her. To connect back to what I had denied. I was aware of the Lord Jesus helping me with this, but this sense of shame of being illegitimate was overwhelming. I wanted to avoid it at all costs. It was obviously a deep shame I had carried all my life and yet I had lived as if there was nothing wrong. The Lord Jesus was showing me the truth that He loved me, wanted me and I was not a mistake, and the Lord had planned for me to be here. He was not ashamed of me, and wanted me to let go of all the shame and pain in my heart for Him to carry. I felt His comfort in a place that was so cold and lonely. I felt His love and compassion warming me, and gradually I let go of all the shame I had carried and received the truth from Jesus that He loved me and was rescuing and restoring me.

As the truth sank in, as I have mentioned, I wanted to bring comfort to that baby that was really me. I began to own that this was my own pain of feeling all alone, unwanted, abandoned at the very start of life. I was convinced I was unwanted, a nuisance, and all I wanted to do was die. However, it was obvious that I did not actually die. I had survived throughout all these years pretending everything was alright and I would have to take care of me. I was beginning to see that I had actually abandoned myself in all the pain, not wanting to feel the agonising loneliness and despair, and determined not to be that person, but to take control to protect myself from being a vulnerable person. That was how I had lived. That meant embracing this baby place in my core and owning the pain and anguish I had so long denied was really mine and could only be met and healed with Jesus. The Bible says that He carried our sorrows and bore our griefs and by His stripes we are healed (see Isaiah chapter 53 verses 4 and 5).

I remember clearly that as I began to live from this place of truth and reality, I was able to begin to nurture and comfort and accept that part of me that I had abandoned long ago in the adoption home. I needed to say sorry to myself for what I had done to avoid feeling all this pain. Thus began the process of feeling the reality of all the loss in my life. It was a hard period, but actually it was very good. I began to feel real for the first time.

Life began to touch me. Things that I would previously have skated over without any emotion or connection now had the capacity to evoke reaction from within. I was beginning to feel, which was a strange. I can only describe it as the feeling of 'pins and needles' in a limb that has been numb for a long while.

Holding a baby, being invited into a family to share Christmas with them, and allowing myself to receive help rather than being fiercely independent... All these events and many more were all touching this empty, isolated place which was so painful, and I can see why previously I had done everything to avoid acknowledging it. The difference now, though, was that as I stayed in the place of connection and acknowledged the pain, a wonderful divine exchange began to take place. As I felt the pain and gave it to Jesus, he poured in His love and truth that He wanted to meet all my needs and take care of me. I cannot describe the wonder of how this began to transform my life. There was hope and acceptance of me for who I really was for the first time in all my sixty-eight years.

The Lord was using everyday events and people around me to touch and gradually melt my frozen heart. I was being loved back into life and it felt good. I began to feel strong, and straighten. As I began to connect up on the inside, my body was reflecting this on the outside. People began to remark on how much energy I had. I felt well, I had even started enjoying being creative, something I always thought of as a waste of time! I was beginning to live like I had never lived before.

This was not all plain sailing. As I was becoming more connected to the truth of all the loss in my life, all sorts of issues and my reactions to them which had long been buried, started to surface. One thing which completely shocked me was one day, without any warning, from the depth of my being, came the words: 'I HATE MY BROTHER!' This was so powerful, I felt overwhelmed. I had never recognised or allowed myself to recognise such a bad statement could exist within me. The way I would have coped with this previously would have been to dismiss it immediately and condemn myself for such a wicked thought. I would judge myself wicked and evil.

So, what was I to do with this? How was I supposed to handle it? It was a bad thought, was it not? So I must be bad? But somehow this was the truth. I knew it to be true, so I must need to bring it out into the light, own it and ask the Lord to help me deal with the huge flow of hatred and anger that I could feel welling up inside me at the thought of my brother. The Lord began to show me all the times my brother had been unkind to me, and I knew I had to come to a place of being willing to forgive him. However, He also showed me the intensity of the hatred was coming from the pain of my illegitimacy, while he was the true son of his parents. I was second class compared to him and that was why I hated him so much.

This was going to take some time to work through, facing the intense emotion, and it was quite a long time after this event that I was finally able to experience a real release from this deep-seated anger and receive a deep healing. We cannot pretend to God, and

He knows everything about us and lovingly and patiently waits until we come to a place of agreement with Him about the truth inside of us. Then He can help us to release the emotion, the anger, the pain, receive the truth of His love, and this brings the peace.

chapter seventeen

DAVID

After our mother's death in 1998, I became more involved with David, as I had promised her that I would, as next of kin, oversee to some degree David's care and any plans that there might be for him. I made more frequent visits to see him and had in mind the injustice in the fact that he had always been required to pay for his stay at the Retreat. I thought this was iniquitous, as you do not have to pay to be in jail. I managed to engage a barrister who was an expert in dealing with these sorts of issues, to review his case and, in conjunction with the family solicitor, we pushed forward to have a review of his status. At that time David was on what is known as 'on section', which meant he could not leave the Retreat and was subject to varying constraints upon his life. I had long believed that when he was brought up for his yearly tribunal, many of which I had attended, that he was drastically over-medicated, to the point that anyone would have felt the need for him to be sectioned.

This day of tribunal was a landmark. The barrister, David's solicitor, David and I were present. The tribunal made a remarkable and courageous decision that he could come off section. On this occasion, David was much less drugged and quite lucid and took part in the discussions with great charm and realism. I was told afterwards by one of the tribunal panel, who I by now knew quite well, that they had no option but to release him, although they did not agree with the decision. That was nine years ago and he is still off section. The next battle was to be with the NHS and social services regarding funding of David's care.

Over the next few years it seemed that David was improving, and he said so himself. I had always thought that when his mother died he would either get radically worse or start to improve, so I was delighted when he did the latter. Our relationship, which as I have said earlier deteriorated steadily over the years as David became more and more ill, slowly improved. Gradually, as I saw more of him and I was less frightened of him, we began to establish a more functional relationship. It was lovely to see glimpses of the charming, engaging person that I knew him to be, which was overlaid by this dreadful illness. Knowing what I had learned from Ellel, maybe I had a more forgiving attitude to him and a greater understanding of how he had descended into this schizophrenic state; his conception was out of wedlock and his traumatic birth, and an upbringing solely by women, surrounded by them with no male figure as a role model meant it was not totally surprising that he struggled, with a stutter and dyslexia. I was also to find out relatively recently that his father was Jewish and in discussions with David he had struggled through life with this confusion of his identity. His failure at teacher training and his bouts of illness had taken their toll on him. After his 'revolving door' years, when his mother could cope no longer and had him put into the Retreat, he would no doubt also have felt a deep sense of abandonment, failure, rejection and lack of self-worth, and no doubt his pain came out in different ways to mine.

After my recent realisation that I had hated David for so many years and blamed him for so much, in robbing me of much in our formative years, it has been really a delight to find I actually want to visit him and to talk about the past. He has a prodigious memory and can fill me in with all the details of holidays and trips here and there and with events in family life which is quite exciting. Having forgiven him, I can now much more easily, and not out of duty, enjoy his company. To this extent, I was able to enjoy arranging for him to have a special birthday party for his seventieth birthday, from which I derived great pleasure; it was a real restoration and an answer to prayer. It appears from hospital reports that he was so overcome by the presents I sent him that he had to retire to his room to recover. I visited shortly thereafter and he was still relating his happy day. I pray for his salvation and greater healing, but leave that to the Lord. I just give thanks for him and for the restoration of our relationship and his healing so far.

There were plans afoot to maybe move him to another facility that the Retreat owned, which was a more homely environment in a small village on the outskirts of York where he could be more part of a local community. I hoped he would not take fright at the thought of moving, after thirty-one years at the Retreat. His usual response to change is to shred his clothes, become shabbier, neglect his personal hygiene and behave more as an inmate of a psychiatric hospital might behave in the hope that he will be seen as needing to stay put. Thankfully, the newer members of staff were no longer frightened of him, nor did they go along with this ploy!

chapter eighteen

MOVING ON

Facing up to one's past and acknowledging it has happened is critical on this journey. It is, in fact, much easier to keep the status quo and keep blaming circumstances, birth, trauma, family, people – anything or anyone who has been part of the damage process throughout life – and continue living a dysfunctional lifestyle. I can only be grateful to those who have challenged me to look beyond the damage, the wrong beliefs I have clung to, the wrong choices I have made, unforgiveness and bitterness I have held onto, and my own sin. That word 'sin' comes as a revelation. I have thought the Ten Commandments relate to obvious sin on things one would try not do and because deep inside one knows that they are wrong. But actually sin is anything which we do that is contrary to God's ways and breaks his laws – unforgiveness and bitterness, grudges held, pronouncements made, self-cursing and wrong beliefs are, when pointed out, so opposite to God's plans and ways. The reality of one's coping mechanisms and the pattern of one's responses when brought in love to one's attention come as a revelation.

Emotions are another area which I have found profoundly difficult to get a grip on. In the early days of ministry, I suspect that I barely allowed any shred of emotion to surface; I had buried so deep anything that might come remotely near being an emotion. I know when I was small and had what DL called 'temper tantrums' she used to call me 'Mussolini' because I would pout. Of course, I had no idea who Mussolini was, but knew whoever he was it was not a compliment. DL thought it very funny. I suspect after that I made a choice not to show any emotion and found it was easier just to ignore them. There were moments, though, when they did surface. When John left me, after a few days there was a great overwhelming uncontrollable crying for several days. I am thankful that I was able to experience and release some of the hurt and pain and grief that was there at that time. On the whole, though, my response to anything traumatic has been to keep on going and say to anyone who might ask, 'I am fine.'

Through the seven years of ministry and learning, it became more and more apparent to me that I had suppressed my emotions. I learned how we need to deal with our emotions in a godly way. It is not that emotions are wrong in any sense. That is how God made us, and we are made in His image and He has emotions, even anger, but it is about how we handle them. It is ungodly to do as I have done all my life and it seems this is what most people do. The only way is to own them and ask God to help one deal with them in a right way. This can be difficult as initially one is not aware that there is this huge untapped well buried inside that is preventing our relationship with God from being as He intended. If we could only grasp that we need to do this on a daily basis, how different our lives would be. Jesus is able, then, to pour in His peace and joy into the place these tangled emotions have lain dormant and festering for years.

Why do we think that we know better about how to run our lives, when God designed us? This is a question that puzzled me for a long time. In reality this is called control, manipulation, arrogance, pride and it is SIN. This word 'sin' none of us like, but in effect it is rebellion to God's ways, disobedience, wrong choices, wrong beliefs, and saying we know better than God. This of course makes us 'god' because we believe we can do better than God; we in effect enthrone ourselves. The recognition of these truths took some time to filter through to me but when I had grasped the depth of these facts I was able to deal with them and renounce, repent and give the emotions to God. I can assure you that that was and is the best decision I have ever made. The outworkings in my life have been profound, and the release has brought with it such a deep sense of peace and joy, which truly does pass all understanding. There is a true sense of peace which is quite different from the false sense of peace I had when I suppressed everything and denied I had any emotions and was in effect in control of my life.

'Rebellion' is the other word which came as a surprise to me – it is clearly linked to disobedience, as one can discover in the dictionary. The dictionary definition is one of open resistance to authority; that says it all, really; the authority in our lives being God and his godly order and His appointed leaders and disciples and our obedience or submission to their authority. (Disciple meaning those under authority; a follower or pupil of a leader.)

Allowing these teachings to enter my spirit and submitting to the will of God in my life has changed me profoundly, and those around me can see that. It was at first difficult for the teaching to go into my spirit as my mind was always reasoning and protecting and interpreting according to what I believed as truth. My healing and understanding of God and his destiny for my life has yet to be fully accomplished as this is a lifelong process, but I thank God that I am well on the way and able to know God's love and acceptance in a way I never did. I am truly thankful and astonished at what I have gained – and not as some people think lost – by giving my life to the Lord. The freedom that has come into my life and the change continues to astound me. It has taken some time for me to truly understand that His ways are not our ways and to embrace my walk with Jesus in a new and different way from the early head knowledge to knowing deep in the core of my being in my spirit that Jesus is Lord.

As time has gone on I realise just how different it is to be whole and not crushed. There is a sense of completeness and wholeness that I have not experienced before, and a joy and excitement not founded on lies or fantasies or driven-ness but of a deep-seated peace and an energy level that I would have thought was almost an impossibility in advancing years. That is not to say I have suddenly become superhuman! But I am not using up energy just to exist and push through in my soul, but can experience an inner peace in the core of my being. I know what it is to be at rest.

chapter nineteen

WISTERIA

A friend asked me to buy a wisteria plant one year for her new pergola, as she had little or no time to go to look for one. I came across one abandoned and alone in the side ward of a garden centre. It was possibly three years old, they said, and had lost its name, its identity, and no one knew what colour it might be. Always liking a bargain, I bought it and brought it home to a somewhat surprised friend – it only just fitted into the quite large car. The abandoned but now treasured plant was given a beautiful pot, and supported on the pergola and the wait for flowers began. The next year she waited for flowers, and the next. Three years later, she was blessed with flowers. Slowly, oh so slowly, the faintest tinge of pink appeared, and as the days went by, a whole pink and white flower. The flowering is the end product of patient care, love, and anticipation of a fullness and completeness. Does God wait patiently for us to come to Him, and is He expectant and excited at the prospect? I think probably so. Somehow this wisteria is a summation of what God has done in my life while being surrounded by love, care, support and godly examples. It has been slow and at times painful and at times glorious, and it is a continuing process. I am still anticipating and expecting more as I continue to walk this path as I gain greater understanding, absorb more truth and develop a closer walk with Father God.

The previous paragraph was to be the final one, but as ever, God has surprises. This latest one was completely unimaginable, and is filling in a whole area that I had no idea would ever be filled. On 9 July 2008, I returned home to find a message on my phone from a lady who said she was my cousin – her father and mine were brothers. She left no phone number, so I dialled 1471 and was given the number. I looked in the phone book and to my amazement she lived on the Isle of Lewis, where my grandfather on my mother's side had owned the Soval estate. I waited for a call the next day as she had said, in the meantime thinking, 'I never knew my father had a brother.' John and Gerald, my half-brothers, had never mentioned uncles.

With great excitement I waited for the call which came early the next day. The lady called Jean rang and said her late father had been called Ronnie. Her father and mine had been brothers along with another called Howard. She had known my father well as a child and later on as an adult. So here, finally, was someone other than my mother who had a limited experience of my father, who could actually tell me about him, his family, and about paternal grandparents. So a whole new chapter began with more family to meet.

Talking on the phone and e-mailing Jean has been quite remarkable. She had obtained my address from Gerald, who had told her that without a doubt I was his father's child. My arrival on the scene had actually caused him great difficulty as his mother was forever accusing my father of his infidelity in front of Gerald, who would have been about thirteen at the time. Therefore, when we had had met in 1987, he and his brother had been somewhat wary of me – apart from the fact that I could have been gold-digging or looking for an inheritance. Gerald has now been able to send to Jean lots of photographs of my father which I had never seen. Jean had stayed with my father's family as a child and has vivid memories of him, and tells me of his wit, charm, and forthrightness, as well as his talent as a very accomplished polo player and excellent horseman.

To have the possibility of meeting another family member but on my father's side was enormously exciting – it would be the icing on the cake. We had already talked about a feeling of belonging even before we had decided that I would visit her in Stornoway in August. It transpired that Jean and her late doctor husband, Ian, had lived for many years in the practice house at Leurbost. This was on the Soval estate that had been at one time owned by my grandfather, and she currently had a plot of land for sale on Soval whilst her daughter owns another home on the estate. The connection on both sides of my family to the Isle of Lewis was quite astounding. Somehow it had always had a pull for me from the time my mother first took me there almost twenty years before. Of course, this would also be an opportunity to climb up the hill on Soval to see where I had scattered Ma's ashes three years ago in pouring rain. I had been unable that day to see the view that she had always talked about, because Ma only showed me the bottom of the hill as she could not climb up to it.

I made arrangements to go to Lewis, staying a night in Ullapool and catching the morning ferry in order to arrive in daytime. I had alerted my grandfather's factor's son, Findley McIver, now in his eighties, to this new turn of events. Of course, he knew Jean's husband Ian as his doctor, and also Jean. I was, however, quite unprepared for what transpired. Jean lives on the road overlooking the sea by the ferry terminal so we had agreed that she would stand outside her door when the ferry docked and I would see her and drive right there. Just as I spotted Jean, I saw someone standing leaning on a car to my left, raising what looked like a stick, and when I looked, to my amazement it was Findley. I stopped the car mid-road, jumped out and said, 'Hello!' We both got into our respective cars and headed for Jean. I had definitely not had this arrival in mind. Jean graciously asked Findley in, and there we were, I meeting my new cousin and Findley with years of stories to tell of my grandfather, aunt, and mother. I heard stories new to me, and who better to tell them than Findley? Finally, Jean asked Findley what my mother was like and he looked straight at me and said, 'You are looking at her.' It was an exciting and somewhat strange meeting, and although it had not been planned was in reality the best possible way of starting my time there. I think God had really gone ahead in this one.

Somewhat delayed but unfazed, Jean produced some lunch, after which we got down to talking in earnest. My brother Gerald had kindly sent Jean a load of photographs of my father and grandparents. I did not know my father had been in the army, but there he was in cavalry uniform with horses. I had previously only had two photos of him, one on a horse and one just standing which were the only treasured photos Ma had of him. Here now in front of me were lots of them, and pictures of my grandparents in their home in Edgbaston. We popped off to the library and had them copied and returned for more stories. Jean had stayed with my father when her parents split up, so she told me about him and Gerald, who is her age. She had also met up with my father as an adult, so she was able to tell me about him as a person. Of course, she could also tell me about her father, the uncle I had never known, and about Howard, my other uncle.

It seemed it was soon time for supper, with a preprandial glass of champagne. A glorious piece of halibut was produced, spanking fresh and delectable, whilst the chatter continued.

We had sensibly planned that I should stay three nights, by which time we felt we should have reached our tolerance level. It seemed that we were having such a good time, and despite Jean dealing with a very painful knee, she made a proposal, that if I would cook the evening meal I could stay the week. This was amazing as Jean does not normally allow anyone in her kitchen, nor does she really have people to stay. So I was indeed honoured and we struck the deal.

The remainder of the week passed so quickly; we went out and about, and Jean was surprised how well I knew the island. I even managed to take her down roads where she had not been, and she showed me new places too. Some of her friends came by, which was good, and we visited the places she knows and loves.

One day I wanted to go up to where I had, with Findley's help, scattered Ma's ashes. I wanted to mark the spot, so I went prepared with one of Ma's treasured cromachs (shepherd's crook) and a hacksaw. The day was glorious, so I parked near to Soval Lodge and started the trek up the hill on very boggy ground. At one point I fell down into a very soggy patch, muttering as the cromach and bag went flying. It was quite a climb for a non-hill walker, but when I reached the spot, which was a very bright green standing out from the surrounding grass, I saw the stunning views in all directions and took some photos.

The intent was to cut the cromach down a bit, dig a hole and insert it and support it with stones. This was accomplished, and it was time to rest and take in the wondrous beauty of creation. There were vistas of the Minch, Loch Soval, the river and, spectacularly, the Harris hills. Wherever the eye roamed was the glory of God.

The trek down was faster, with a few stumbles, but the car was reached and it was time to explore.

I went down a road I had not been along before and almost immediately saw a lady carrying some bags, so I stopped to see if I could give her a lift. She asked if I was on holiday to which I replied, 'Not exactly.' I said my grandfather was Henry Thornton, who had owned Soval. She said she had never met him but had heard he was a good landowner and had allowed people to cut turf on the estate instead of having to go up onto the common. I then said I was staying with Jean who was Ian McIntosh's widow. The riposte to that was: 'We will never have another doctor like him.' We chatted on about the area and the village she lived in and how life is today, and then we parted. I thought how extraordinary it was to pick someone up and hear positive comments about two of my island connections.

My early and daily trip seemed to revolve around the excellent fishmonger near to Jean's home. It was there I was able to obtain the freshest and choicest of fish for our nightly repast. My last day, I wanted to find some fish to bring home, so we both visited and I was asked when I would be back.

I wanted very much to spend some time with Findley and Marie, his wife, on my own, as I had previously been with my mother or my cousin Sheila, my Aunt Monica's daughter who helped me to scatter Ma's ashes. We arranged that I would visit them and so I drove out to Laxay and spent a wonderful few hours being provided with home-baked goodies and hearing more stories, again some I had not heard. We talked about my grandfather and his management of the estate, his fishing, and the people who had stayed at the lodge. I told Findley I had lots of my grandfather's salmon and trout flies, some of which he had tied himself. The Gaffer, as Ma called her father, used to drive up from Somerset with his entourage, including some cockerels from whose feathers he used to tie flies. I said I would send them to him when I got home. I had also brought photographs of my mother's from the Soval days and he was able to name the dogs, the cockerels, and discuss the pictures of the day's catch of salmon. This all went towards my feeling increasingly rooted and grounded, what with my new-found cousin and the tales of my grandfather. Findley and his wife had been converted in the 1949 revival on Lewis and were able to tell me about the night the revival meeting was held at Soval Lodge where, of course, Findley was born and brought up. I asked if they could tell me more about the revival, to which they answered in unison, 'It's too precious to share.'

Time was running out and the return to the mainland was approaching. I was catching the midday ferry to Ullapool with a head full of all that had happened, but also my spirit had been touched in a way at that time I could not verbalise as it too was 'too precious'.

Jean was turning eighty in early October and had told me about the black tie dinner her daughter was throwing for her and the family at her home in Amesbury, Wiltshire. This was a family-only do, no boyfriends! She was excited about the upcoming event, which was not far away. Suddenly a week before the event Jean phoned and asked if I would go, and the instant answer was, 'Yes, please.' It's a long way to Amesbury from where I live and black tie dinners are not frequent occurrences in my life; I did not own what might be described as 'black tie gear'!

A sudden visit to clothes shops in the vicinity came up with two fairly different outfits, both acquired. Then a quick call was made to see if I could stay with my cousin Sheila in Winchester, just down the road from Amesbury. There was a quick booking of a hotel in Amesbury for the night of the party, and a plan for the journey was hatched. This was complicated by the fact that I was selling my car and having a small motorhome converted in Huddersfield. The plan was to drive to Huddersfield, pick up a loan car and immediately head south towards Winchester. I picked up a weird Honda unknown in this country, and set off south on the M1 feeling a bit insecure about the whereabouts of wipers, lights and so on. On the outskirts of Oxford I knew I had reached my limit, after some eleven hours of driving. A motorway hotel was the answer for the night, and then early down to Winchester for breakfast!

A day of recovery and some time to explore more of Winchester with Sheila was undertaken, and then on to a dinner party at Sheila's for a few people. Next day it was time to get ready to go down to Amesbury, check into the hotel and get organised to meet the family. The only person of the nine people who would be there that I knew was, of course, the birthday lady herself, Jean. I had found the house where I was to go, in daylight, so as not to add any complications to the evening, trying to find where to go in the dark. So now yet again I was to go through the process of meeting unknown family. Having survived this process quite a few times, I had decided there was no point in getting in a stew about it, so just got on with the preparations.

Maybe I was so mechanical about it all so that if it was a disaster I would not get hurt or feel rejected. I remember sitting on the bed in my finery being quite unemotional about it all, thinking, 'I have been through this before with my half-brothers, my mother, my cousin Sheila and, of course, Jean herself. So why will this be any more scary, except for the number of people?' I got into the car, offered a quick prayer, and then I was off up the road. I parked, took a deep breath and opened the car door. As I did so, Isobel, Jean's daughter, with umbrella, and her husband, Nick, came to the car and escorted me to their home. They explained that I was not going to be greeted by all of the family at once, but to go in to meet Jean, have some champagne, and the rest would come in, as and when, to join us for a pre-dinner drink. That was a relief, as maybe I would get all the names straight then! The evening was crowned by a wonderful dinner, with the opportunity to talk to everyone at some point. After dinner provided more opportunities to meet and share. What an amazingly diverse family with so many talents in such different subjects! One of the poignant times for me was the photographs, where I was right in the middle of the family, accepted and belonging. I had been greeted with cards of welcome to the family, but this really went deep. There was no question of my heritage as an illegitimate person, but a depth of welcome and inclusion that I still find difficult to verbalise.

Isobel kindly took me back to my hotel and invited me for breakfast, saying she would pick me up in the morning. What a sleep I had! I woke early to get organised for the day. I spent all day, breakfast and then an early supper/late lunch, with all of them. It was a truly precious time and felt so right. I returned to Winchester to regale Sheila with the events, before heading for home the following day. The journey home in two days provided plenty of time for reflection, and this has been ongoing till this juncture of writing about the momentous year of meeting with a family I had no idea existed.

The other truly unexpected event to round the year off was that David did move, with very little protestation, to the satellite facility in York, mentioned earlier. I had been to see his new room-to-be a few weeks before, and was able to meet with him the day before he moved, on my way to yet another family do – in Winchester this time. He had seemed perhaps resigned to the inevitable, but there was a sort of dignified excitement about him. I phoned to see if his transplant after thirty-one years had happened, and it had, evidentially without a hitch. I visited him five days afterwards to find him cosily ensconced in his new room, probably the nicest he had ever had, facing south on the ground floor. David had already been on the bus to check the village out.

Truly, this again I had hardly dared to think could happen, certainly with the ease that it did. He executed the move with the good grace that his mother did when she found herself incarcerated in nursing homes. I think God had again made a way. My ongoing prayer is for his salvation.

chapter twenty

MORE MINISTRY

At some point, some six and a half years after I had joined the Blairmore team, it seemed right to ask for another session of ministry. There were still some issues surrounding the deprivation which I had adamantly refused to face for all the time I was at Blairmore. I felt the Lord say, 'You need to own that and deal with the pain of it.' This 'deprivation' word was the one that Anna had used early on in my time on-team. I knew this was the time that I was finally ready to face the reality of my early years and the pain associated with them.

Early into the ministry time, I said I thought maybe it would be good to go to the creativity room, a dedicated place where there are numerous supplies of all kinds of materials to allow all sorts of creative activity and exploration, or just to be free to make a mess. I had seen many people through the years have deep, deep healing by just allowing God to work in their spirits and bypass their often overactive minds. I had also come to the place where just playing or making a mess or creating something was no longer a threat, as it had been initially.

So up we went and I asked God what He wanted to show me. To my amazement I picked up a brush and began a fairly diagrammatic sketch, mostly in black, of the home I was brought up in. Interestingly, my bedroom had a black window, as did the summer house where I spent a lot of time alone, and my little patch of garden was not pretty. Then, from what one might say nowhere, came the word 'deprived', written in bold black letters. Then a stream of other words – 'abused, slave, controlled, used, rejected, fatherless, shame, lonely, isolated, self-rejected, abandoned'. This was at last me being able to write the truth down of what my life had been. I was astounded, to say the least; these words had come from my spirit, not my head, and this was the reality I had to face.

I happened to know where a great wedge of clay was and there was suddenly a huge swell of anger rising within me which I knew had to be expressed in a godly way. This was righteous anger at what had happened, and it needed to come out. I got a huge chunk of clay and started throwing it with all the force I had onto the floor, picking it up and doing it again. I was not throwing it at anyone or for a particular event, but it somehow unleashed from deep inside me a release of all that pent-up and buried anger. This felt so good, and then I stood on my picture and stamped all over it, almost in an attempt to obliterate it because the past had now been acknowledged. The reality had been admitted, and it could now be put behind me. Not that I would not think of the reality of the events any more, but the pain and emotion associated with them had no power to hold me or allow the enemy to taunt me.

As I had to face the truth that I was unwanted, unplanned, unloved, and an inconvenience, it had made me feel I was wrong, worthless, a reject, and that I was unlovable. I felt unsafe and there was no one to meet my needs. My reaction to this feeling inside was: 'I will show you! I will succeed, I will be self-sufficient.' I had, in fact, rejected and abandoned myself. My heart cry was always, 'I just want to be loved.'

Then had to come the repentance and forgiveness from this new understanding. I had to connect to the pain and forgive myself for abandoning myself. This again was a process, and painful.

I suppose that day was a watershed in my healing, as at long last I had accepted the reality of my past life. It was, of course, then the opportunity for the Lord to flag up some more issues over time which I was now more able to deal with in a godly manner, just me and God. This now means that my ongoing walk is not determined by how soon I can have another ministry time, but how quickly I can recognise the issue, forgive others, myself, repent, renounce and bring the issue to the cross.

chapter twenty one

SOMERSET

In the summer of 2010 I was able to go down to Somerset with Sheila, who has a housing charity down there. It was an opportunity to meet again with my half-brother Gerald, my father's younger son, and possibly a time where I could meet him on my own and hear more about my father and uncles. Sheila and I drove down in my campervan and had arranged to meet Gerald at the Lion Hotel in Dulverton, a small village on the edge of Exmoor. My father had run the livery and hunting stable of the Lion Hotel, and my cousin had met him there with her mother as a child. She, of course, had known Gerald too, but not seen him for years.

I was not really expecting anything exceptional from the meeting, but was suddenly a bit overwhelmed to be in a place where my father had been a regular, well known and respected. Gerald could tell me stories of my father and show me where he had sat with his ever-present dog. It was also a first to be in the company of both sides of my family at once, which was a new idea to process. I so wanted Gerald and Sheila to like each other, which thankfully they did, so we had a very jolly lunch together. I found myself asking if our father did this or that, which sounded quite alien to me, never having really talked about 'a father'. Also, Gerald gave me a sort of sketch of my grandparents. My grandfather was a vet in Solihull with a speciality in horses which had been very vital in the First World War, training and caring for the remount horses, those which replaced the killed or injured ones.

I had taken Sheila to the train in Taunton, and had intended to leave the next day, but somehow it felt right to stay on as the weather was glorious. I wanted to see Gerald again and explore on my own some of the places I had been before with my mother. Also, I needed to really get to know the small village and walk about up and down and in and out of places I had heard about.

I booked into the little campsite in the village which offered me the very spot to walk about and really get a feel of the place. I met with all sorts of people who had known my grandfather, and that was satisfying too, as I had only heard of him before on the Isle of Lewis in his fishing mode. I got a real sense of the man and his hunting prowess, and more of a sense of him as a person. I was also able to visit Gerald at his home, which was even more profound as he was able to show me our father's pictures, war medals and letters of appreciation from some very interesting people. Although one might think Dulverton is in the back of beyond, because of the stag hunting, many people from far and wide landed there, and inevitably came across my father. Somehow this visit gave me a sense of closure to the finding of my mother. It really rounded off what had been a life-changing experience – that of meeting my real mother.

The weather continued to be exceptional as I toured around Exmoor and revisited places I had been previously. However, to be there and have the time to process the whole episode of my roots was an immensely healing time.

The time is quickly approaching to celebrate three score years and ten, which is a fine opportunity to rewind and see how the intervention and guiding hand of God has been there all throughout my life, although I was unaware of it until I made Jesus the Lord of my life. Much of the journey was lived in darkness, in rebellion and in sin. It's been a tortuous and winding adventure in many ways. God has been so faithful and has gently taught me about His kingdom, and given me opportunities to share my journey with others who have had to face difficult journeys as well. He has, as have others, shown me unconditional love, encouraged me, laughed and cried with me, and allowed me to make mistakes. We truly do serve an awesome God.

To God be the glory.

APPENDIX

Précis of Diana's letter to her sister 15/01/89

Dear Monica

I thought I gave you somewhat of a surprise yesterday when I told you about my daughter and that I ought to give you some information about her background and upbringing.

I call her Gillian as that is the name I gave her, but she was brought up as a Quaker in Co. Durham and went to a very good Quaker school in York.

Then she went to Oxford to train as an OT – they cope with handicapped and geriatric people as regards aids and house conversions. After that she went to Canada and met and married a man 20 years older than her with two teenage sons. They were married 23 years but he took off last year to Canada as the age gap was telling. Actually I think he was more geriatric than me!

It has been a great thing for me and livened up my old age enormously. Though it was not easy at first telling people around here about it and a few others, it had to be done because apparently we are so alike, though I cannot see it. Fortunately everyone we have so far told has been so pleased and happy for us …

NOTES MADE BEFORE, DURING AND AFTER THE SEARCH FOR MY MOTHER.

The idea of actually looking for my mother was precipitated by DL on my birthday in 1987. I asked if she had any information on my proper mother, not a good choice of words. The reply was I have thrown them all out.

I had not done so before for fear of opening a can of worms, and having divided loyalties, and why complicate life. But DL was 87, my husband had left, my brother was a schizophrenic so I had no family into my old age.

I wanted to know the family history, need to know, to feel, to touch, to know why I am the way I am, what is inherited and what is environmental.

Always interested in a mother not a father, probably easier to cope with a mother as I don't know a lot about fathers. Did not want to deal with illegitimacy, actually when a friend mentioned the word I was horrified.

20/08/87

My social worker hands me a type written note describing my mother, and the fact that my father had admitted paternity. Then I was given some handwritten notes that my mother had written … almost cracked up. I did after she left.

10/09/87

Must write things down. Relief excitement and the realisation that this may be all I get. How to find more? An idea came to go down to Dulverton and look at gravestones, maybe find grandparents and go from there.

Shall I tell DL? No, she would not cope. Will it alter my feelings for her? And if so how/subtlety [sic] or overtly? How might it affect my life? Can I deal with it?

What do I want? Photos, treasures, family history, roots, relatives, people who care? Family traits.

Did my mother ever think of me? Did she have regrets, sadness, trauma, what did I do for her life? How did she feel[,] how did she cope in 1941?

7/10/87

At 10am tomorrow I shall come eyeball to eyeball with my mother. How will I react, what will she look like, will she like me? Will we get on? What has she had to clam up about all this time? How does she feel? What will I find about me? I think I already know, I'll love her. Will this be a different kind of love to the kind I have for DL?

Help there is no textbook for this kind of thing. No one can tell you how to do it.

How much of me is my mother[;] why do I act the way I do?

Has she run away from herself and the past? Nearly 50 years have elapsed. Maybe this will be the first person who will truly understand me. What about emotion[,] surely we will have to deal with that, we can't just say hello, let's go birdwatching!

Diana keeps using the word roots[;] she seems to sense that is what I need, though I had not really thought that.

Really hardly dare think about tomorrow, will we find we can relate or is this an exercise in futility?

What will this do to her life and mine, the reality is neither of us will be the same again whatever the outcome.

What else can I say to Diana but thank you. I have had a wonderful life whatever that means and you gave me life.

Did you ever cry alone? Did you ever wonder what happened to me and what I had done with my life? Could you love me?

What did I want[,] why did I do this? I suppose it was to find my roots and what does that mean? A sense of belonging to some other human being not just an attachment to be picked up and put down on demand.

Do I hug her, shake hands or say 'Hello nice to meet you'? This will probably be the most exciting moment of my life.

She must be unusual to be able to process all this stuff in 3 days and to meet me. Dare I cry? I pray she won't change her mind and say she can't go through with this. 1300 miles over 3 days to have this moment.

She doesn't like people much, likes to be different, to shock. Talking to her is like talking to someone one has known all your life, which of course it is.

Never realised how important it might be to have someone who understand me. Maybe I will not be tortured any more.

08/10/87

Is this really happening or is it a dream? This has been the longest night ever and soon very soon the moment of truth.

10 AM precisely the blue Subaru parked outside the hotel and I watched as she got out. Two minutes later as she came through the door I suddenly see my own eyes looking at me. She came in and said 'How are you' and a kiss. Small and plump, big bosom, certainly not mine!! She immediately said 'Oh you have your fathers eyes and nose and legs!

She talked for 11 hours almost without looking at me in the car and in the hotel. She said I would have been a battered baby and she had tried to get rid of me with gin and a knitting needle. She came as she said as she is, what a dear eccentric. She talked like she had known me for years and I knew everyone. Talked about Bill, her one real love who she had known most of her life. I asked if she ever thought of me and a resounding NO came out how could you she said.

Wanted to know how I felt about having a crest and coat of arms.

She had brought the family tree and books on the family with pictures all a bit much to absorb in a day. She accepted an invitation to have dinner with me and left for home about an hour away. She said she wanted to be called Ma and she wanted to call me Gillian.

No plans were made as we parted but early next morning a call asking me to call in on my way back to York. So she showed me her tiny home and her treasures. She talked more about Bill and said she had known him since she was 16 and saw him before he died, said it was 'not one jump in the air' said she did not feel much. After two hours I left and cried all the way to York.

Although we did not make plans then we knew we would continue the relationship.

13/09/87

Still magical though I worry what I may have caused for Ma. Now the reality how to deal with John, DL and Ma. Had a call from Ma[;] its slowly sinking in with her too, says she is coping well and said how happy she is about it, but it is difficult to come to terms with. She wants to know more about me, said I will do a potted history. Said she going [sic] to Devon for her 75th birthday and doesn't come via York so it may be a while till we meet, but we can write and phone as we explore our relationship.

THE AUTHOR

Angela was born in 1941 to an unmarried mother who had tried unsuccessfully to abort her, and given up for adoption some nineteen days after her birth. The adoptive home had all the trappings of wealth and care, but love and a father were the missing ingredients, as the nurture was mainly given by a series of nannies.

The major events in Angela's life were the searching for and finding of her biological mother in 1987, which was a profound milestone. This event brought with it a family tree, half-brothers, cousins and a whole blood family, a revelation to Angela. Here was a history and genealogy which Angela had never dreamed could happen, nor could she have imagined the impact it would have upon her.

The second and life-changing event was Angela making Jesus Lord of her life.

This decision totally transformed her life and it is this part which is written about in the later part of the book.